33
SYCAMORE

*To Mike

A great Everpresent

Best Wishes

Dale*

A SEARCH FOR RECOGNITION

DALE R. LYONS
AUTOBIOGRAPHY

Copyright © 2012 by Dale R. Lyons.

Library of Congress Control Number: 2012910879
ISBN: Hardcover   978-1-4771-3004-9
               Softcover   978-1-4771-3003-2
               Ebook   978-1-4771-3005-6

All rights reserved. No part of this book may be reproduced or transmitted in any form or by any means, electronic or mechanical, including photocopying, recording, or by any information storage and retrieval system, without permission in writing from the copyright owner.

This book was printed in the United States of America.

To order additional copies of this book, contact:
Xlibris Corporation
0-800-644-6988
www.xlibrispublishing.co.uk
Orders@xlibrispublishing.co.uk

CONTENTS

Introduction 9

Chapter 1   The War Years & Growing Up, 1937-1948 11
Chapter 2   Whitley Bay & North Shields Education, 1948-1952 26
Chapter 3   Early Jobs & Leaving For London, 1953-1958 37
Chapter 4   National Service in the Royal Air Force, 1958-1961 52
Chapter 5   A Start in Catering Management, 1961-1962 65
Chapter 6   The American Experience—Emigration to
             The USA, 1962-1965 69
Chapter 7   Senior Catering Management UK, 1965-1970 85
Chapter 8   Moving into Further & Higher Education, 1970-1977 94
Chapter 9   The Open University Years, 1970-1990 101
Chapter 10   Skiing—A New Sport & Partners, 1975-2010 106
Chapter 11   The Birmingham Experience, 1978-1988 120
Chapter 12   Consultancy & lecturing, 1988-2002 134
Chapter 13   Marathon Mania, 1979-2011 142
Chapter 14   Rugby & Rotary Experiences, 2000-2008 168
Chapter 15   Back to Birmingham, 2008-2011 178
Chapter 16   Reminiscences of My Dad—Joseph Robinson Lyons 182
Chapter 17   Final Thoughts 190

Appendix 1   My Daughters' Memories 197
Appendix 2   Marathon Reports, 1981-2011 204

For my resolute Dad and Mam, who died before I could really appreciate her; my two beautiful daughters, Kyla and Iona; my four sprightly grandchildren—Joe, Marisa, Anna, and Niamh; son-in-law Simon; my running buddies, Geoff and Colin, for prompting my suspect memory; and for Janet, my long-time partner, who was my conscience and touchstone throughout and her family—Daniel, Susannah, Olivia, Amelia, Patrick and Jo.

Introduction

Why did I decide to write an autobiography? Initially, it was a challenge initiated three years ago by a New Years resolution list, which had in turn been taken from a 'bucket list' drawn up after seeing a film of the same name starring Jack Nicholson and Morgan Freeman. Also, when I passed seventy years, increasing thoughts of my own mortality crept into life's equation, and I felt inspired to leave, for my family, something tangible of a time and of experiences they had little knowledge or understanding of. I also wanted to show them and anyone else interested that someone from a working class background with restricted opportunities could succeed given the will and motivation.

Perhaps my achievements described in the following pages will provide some evidence that I have made a fist of my search for recognition, for example, completing B.A. and M. Sc degrees on a part-time basis and becoming a University lecturer.

It is also designed to show, albeit in a limited way, that my failed attempts to become a reporter could have blossomed, given the opportunity. And to show that individuals labelled 'reject' by a flawed educational system could rise above that burden to a senior management level.

This search for self recognition through achievement is really what has driven me to write this autobiography.

I have tried throughout to describe some of the memorable elements of my life and times in a way that has some detail, accuracy, and entertainment value.

Its completion will to some extent help me to understanding what, through the years has driven me forward.

CHAPTER 1

THE WAR YEARS & GROWING UP, 1937-1948

Me at 4 months with Mam age 36 Alston 1937.

With Dad in Alston Cumbria on the Archer's farm 1937 age 4 months—notice he has two legs!

Early Days in Beverley Road

It was a gleaming shiny monster, which roared like a lion and belched fumes and smoke outside our house in Beverley Road. The newest Rudge Ulster motorbike was Dad's pride and joy in 1939. My earliest memory was of sitting precariously on the bike and being wheeled up and down the cul-de-sac with my Mam looking on unhappily and agitated. I was two years old, and World War 2 was months away.

Dad had a top job as head waiter at the posh Rex Hotel in Whitley Bay where all the Division 1 football teams stayed when playing Newcastle United. Mam had a part-time job at Dobsons grocery shop near to Bygate School, where my sister Cherry and brother Bernard went. Cherry was 8 years and Bernard 6 years older, so I was the afterthought and, by their reckoning, 'spoilt rotten'. Not, I hasten to add without good reason because I was a handsome and likable little boy. Born as I was on the 26th February 1937 in the Frater Maternity Home, North Shields to Mary Josephine Lyons and Joseph Robinson Lyons, the 2nd son of Joseph and Mary. Was there some religious significance in this event I wonder?

Me as a Senior Sixer boy scout in the Hillheads Troop Age 9 1946.

Disaster Strikes The Family

I was two years old in 1939 with the war only days away. Dad had been returning from work at the Rex Hotel late on a Sunday night to North Shields in October 1939 on his motorbike. Passing the Park Hotel at Tynemouth on the seafront, a car without lights came out of Beach Road without stopping and crashed into the bike, hurtling him across the road. The car did not stop, and Dad, seriously injured and barely conscious, had to instruct two passers-by to put a tourniquet on his thigh as an artery had been severed. His broken femur (thigh bone) had torn through his clothes with the impact. Eventually a St. John's Ambulance team took him to Preston Hospital in North Shields for an emergency operation and finally to Newcastle General. The surgeons gave him little hope of survival due to the trauma, shock, and loss of blood. It was later revealed that because of the poorly applied tourniquet, gangrene had to be cut away three times until the whole leg had to be removed up to his hip. His life hung in the balance for weeks. The attendant surgeons and doctors were astounded that he survived and put it down his spirit and mental strength—there was little else to help! Some relations 'cheered' him up on visits to the hospital saying that he could always become a nightwatchman!

Moving Down Market to 33 Sycamore Avenue

Dad eventually recovered minus one left leg and lost his job at the Rex. There was not much call for a one-legged head waiter. Once Dad recovered, our finances were insufficient to stay in Beverley Road, and so we moved to a council house only one street away at 33 Sycamore. Although it had three bedrooms and a garden, it was a cramped and cheerless place for a toddler. I did, however, get a durable plaything on the kitchen lino floor. While Mam did the washing, I would crawl into the kitchen and use the iron stove's handle to help me up, and once up, I would rattle the handle up and down. One day, my Dad saw me doing this exercise, and when I sat down exhausted, he took the stove door off, so I could continue rattling the handle. Who needs posh toys?

Dad's undaunted spirit, coupled with a newly minted false leg from Roehampton gained him work as a government inspector for munitions factories across England. To get the job he was a little economical with the truth in relation to his qualifications. Nevertheless, he did a good job travelling the country now at war, rejecting slipshod manufacturing of bomb tails, glider controls, and assorted munitions. He was roundly astonished at the cost cutting of avaricious factory owners, who would have endangered our own troops by using sub-standard materials! They didn't get by my Dad!

33 Sycamore Avenue Hillheads, Whitley Bay my home from 1940 after Dad lost his leg. A drab but cosy council house. Has seen better days! 2002.

War Time Street Games

My initial war-time memories are fragmented. But I can still remember the back garden, Anderson bomb shelters, and the smell of paraffin lamps and the damp earth even now! One evening in 1941, when I was four, my brother Bernard, decided that a night in a tent in the back garden would be good fun. At about 2 a.m. however, the wail of the air-raid warning blasted through the canvas opening. We made the bomb shelter just before the crackle and thump of the German bombs obliterated houses only two streets away. No more tented nights after that!

Bath night Friday was shared, and being the smallest, I was also the last in. Same water only murkier and cooler. Looking out of the bathroom window, the searchlights picked up a German bomber, a Dornier my brother said as he was into model building. Suddenly a parachute dropped from the plane and slowly drifted down, two to three miles away as we discovered. It wasn't, as we thought, a pilot baling out but a landmine set to detonate above ground for maximum damage. It made a direct hit on All Saints' parish church in Cullercoats and killed the organist. Wags later said he had been practising 'Nearer my god to thee' at the time. A good example of wartime humour!

I started school when I was four years old because Mam had a part-time job. My first activity was to play in the sandpit, and later the next day, I was accosted by a rather forward young lady with red hair of five years called Brenda who sat on me until I kissed her. I wonder what happened to Brenda! With parents working, we had to make our own way home from school, even at the tender age of five! Mind you, it was only a quarter mile or so, but often I'd get caught short and had to make a speedy entrance through the back window so as not to be disgraced. At the bottom of our garden grew lots of micklemas daisies, attracting assorted bees in the summer. My favourite pastime was snatching the bees from the flower heads and listening to them buzzing imprisoned in my tiny fist. This innocent and inexpensive pastime unfortunately lasted until a particular bee's patience ran out. I found out too late that pain avoidance motivation is true! I never played with the bees and daisy heads again!

Another innocent though potentially hazarded amusement, though we didn't know at the time was playing on the local tip, conveniently located at the end of Sycamore Avenue. Health and safety issues, controls, and regulations were fortunately far in the distant future, so we six-year old scavengers collected anything remotely interesting. My memorable find, at the time, was an almost unused tube of lipstick, which I wrapped in coloured paper and presented to my sister on her fourteenth birthday. Knowing I had zero funds, she enquired as to its pedigree and was incensed to find out where it had originated. Personally I was cut to the quick at such ingratitude.

My first cat was called Dusky, a beautiful light grey shorthaired Tom. When I was six Dusky damaged his paw which became poisoned, probably on the same rubbish tip. As we had little money for vets bills he had to be put down and the cost at that time was half a crown (12.5p). My Dad gave me the money and told me to take Dusky to the vet. You grew up quickly in those days!

Dangers in the Street

Of course, during the war, the most sort after possessions were pieces of shrapnel or bomb fragments, the bigger the better. After an air-raid we could roam bombed-out houses without let or hindrance, searching for the elusive prize pieces or just play about in the debris.

The smell of burnt, water-soaked bedding and furniture is a lasting memory. Hazards were a daily but unappreciated risk until reality kicked in. Street drains also were a particular attraction. Things, sometime valuable, fell down drains such as prize marbles. Lifting heavy cast-iron covers required concerted teamwork for five—to six-year olds. On one occasion, I volunteered to delve into the sludge for marbles but didn't remove my hand quick enough. The cover proved too heavy for the 'team', and the edge sliced through my left hand's middle finger, second joint. The scar remains to this day as a reminder but my finger survived.

Lesson 1. 'Don't mess with drains!'

About the same time, I became violently allergic to marrows, cucumbers, or anything in that vegetable family, which lasted into my twenties. Returning from Bygate infant school one day in the summer whilst investigating a hedgerow, we found to our delight some vegetable marrows, and naturally during the war, we were always hungry. It didn't take long to devour as much marrow as our little tummies could manage. Whether it was the amount we ate or their over-ripeness or perhaps they had been discarded as bad I'll never know. The resulting agonising stomach ache and sickness created this long-time aversion.

Lesson no. 2: Don't eat found items however attractive!

Have you ever attempted to swallow a halfpenny (now a 2 p piece)? It's not a good idea when you're only six years old. I made this attempt sitting in the back of Mrs Coates's class at Bygate infants and 'showing off' to Barbara Fellows. Actually I wasn't trying to swallow it—just pretending—but it went further than intended. 'Dale's swallowed a halfpenny', cried Barbara to the teacher. Gagging and spluttering, I was rushed to the head teacher and taken to the nearest doctor in Ocean Drive Whitley Bay. Another teacher was sent to Grocer Dobson's to fetch my Mam. An abortive attempt by the doctor to remove the coin, which fortunately for me had stuck vertically in my windpipe, was followed by a frantic ambulance ride to Preston (North Shields) hospital. Had the coin stuck horizontally, Dale would not have reached double figures! After many bitten doctors fingers later it was decided the only place for coin removal was Newcastle Infirmary. We are now in mid-afternoon and four pints of water later as they rushed me into surgery and a general anaesthetic. My only memory was a dream that like Quasimodo in the Cathedral tower was hearing a chorus of bells. I then woke up to find the dreaded coin under my pillow and a relieved mother stroking my hair.

Lesson 3: Don't show off swallowing halfpennies in class—or anywhere else for that matter. For months after, I suffered from sore throats as a consequence.

Sycamore Avenue was a short distance to lots of exciting but potentially dangerous places. One of these was an abandoned mine of unknown minerals, probably coal, which was supposed to go all the way to the coast and emerge at Cullercoats Bay about three miles away. We would play 'dares' to see who could go farthest inside. As we didn't have torches, it was probably only a few yards before we frightened ourselves into the daylight again. Cullercoats was one of our favourite beaches for swimming and exploring and surprisingly remains almost the same today almost 70 years on.

Choir Boys are Sissies!

I did not want to be a choir boy. My Dad who never went to church insisted we became regular Christians with morning prayers, Sunday school singing 'Jesus wants me for a sunbeam', and the evening service as well. Other attractions held greater magnetism, especially when my non-choir boy friends were free to play. On one of these days playing truant from the choir, I attempted to generate some income from a telephone box by pressing Button B. This ruse of extracting monies left over from callers too rushed to care operated on the basis of the psychological element called 'intermittent reinforcement'. Your reward of a few pennies from this activity might only happen 1 % of the time spent, but we kept hoping nevertheless. On this particular Sunday morning, I and Brian Heads, my best friend, were so engrossed in pressing Button B that we never saw a man approaching neatly attired with a walking stick. Yes, you have guessed; it was my Dad. I was so traumatised I can't remember either the rebuke or the punishment, but probably he docked my pocket money for two weeks. This amounted to 3 p (old money) weekly—about 1.5 p decimal. That was two Mars Bars worth and a lot to lose!

A reluctant choir boy at St. Peter's Church
Monkseaton. Age 11. 1948.

Dad—The Entertainer and Economiser

Dad however had another string to his bow—party entertainer! On my 9th birthday, he organised the food and fun for my ten guests and with his somewhat suspect ideas of fun filled some of the sausage rolls with balsa wood! Two other 'tricks' followed: the first involved taking one of his fast diminishing hairs and placing it in a saucer of water with the instructions to 'watch very carefully and when I say the magic words the hair will stand on end'. Naturally we all came close to watch the phenomenon, and as he finished the magic phrase, his hand smacked into the saucer spraying everyone. 'Did you see it?' asked my laughing Dad as we wiped the water from our collective eyes. 'No? Ah, well you didn't get close enough' was the response.

The best trick however was to take a glass of water, place a round bar tray on top, and on the tray place a wine cork with a penny piece on top of the cork. 'Now, how can I get that penny into the glass without touching the penny, the cork, or the glass?' He would ask. After five minutes getting nowhere with the answer, then racking up the excitement, he told us to stand back. He hit the tray smartly with his palm; the tray hit the cork, and the penny dropped neatly into the water glass—job done to resounding applause from the amazed youngsters.

His party piece though was to lay a table with cutlery, plates, cups and saucers and ask how can I take the cloth away without touching the cutlery, plates, cups or saucers? When we gave up he would whip the cloth away with a flourish leaving the cutlery and crockery in place. A trick honed to perfection in his years as a waiter.

As a gullible nine years old, every year he would say to me on 31 December, 'Dale, today you will see a man who has as many noses as there are days in the year,' and when I came home later would ask me if I had seen that man. It wasn't until later when I stopped believing in Santa Claus that I knew the answer. Do you?

During the war when money was scarce, he would repair all our shoes, and I remember one Christmas when he made me a rail engine big enough for me to sit on. What a Dad!

My Travels with Granny Tearse

Mam's mother Granny Tearse lived in North Shields and would often take me on visits to her relatives. One of these was a cousin who lived in a tall house in Low Fell, which was part of Gateshead just to the South of Newcastle. We took the tram from Newcastle's Northumberland Street and rattled over the Tyne Bridge for about twenty-five minutes. I remember having tea and cakes and being allowed out to the local Saltwell Park where they had the most enormous banana slide—I was seven years old so it probably just seemed enormous. On another occasion, we went to Granny's friend who lived in Warrington. I don't remember the journey or much of the visit except I decided to go walk-a-bout, promptly got lost, and almost created an organised search by the local police before finding my way back.

A lasting memory was visiting the Blackpool Illuminations when I was about six years old, cramped into the well of a Ford Anglia fast asleep on the return journey. I don't remember the lights though! Granny must have liked my company, because we often went to the cinema in North Shields. One film I do remember was *Major Barbara*, which was about the tough life of a salvation army lady. It was a very gloomy film and quite frightening too. Granny Tearse was an Savaltion Army regular, and I've a photo of her, one of very few in her army bonnet and overcoat. I still remember and recount much of her home spun philosophy that had more than a grain of truth in it. Answering my complaint that some bread was hard she would say, 'it's harder where there is none!' and, asking where the gravy was with a particular meal, would say 'hunger's the best sauce, my lad!' Another expression she would use when being uncomplimentary to someone she considered too thin was 'I've seen more fat on a greasy chip'.

When I was eighteen, Granny Tearse died at the age of eighty-two, living in condemned buildings in Northumberland street, her husband whom I never met died in his forties.

I was quite disgusted that my Aunty Millie, her other daughter, had taken no responsibility for her when she became unable to cope, even though their house in Howden had plenty of spare accommodation.

Granny Tearse, Mam's mother 1940 a keen Salvationship who took me on many trips and loved condensed milk in her tea!

Granddad Tearse who I never met about 1905.
Mam's Dad died in his early 40's.

My Street Buddies and Enemies

Martin Chiswell was about my age and lived directly opposite us in Sycamore Avenue. He rarely came out and never played with us because his mother did not consider us suitable playmates. She was a single mother and a bit of a snob. We would see him at his upstairs window and make faces at him. One main reason for our belligerence was that at Christmas during the war, he always had had lots of expensive presents, which, of course, he never shared with us. I often wonder what become of Martin Chiswell.

On another occasion Brian Heads who lived next door was throwing darts in the local park when one went up in the air off line and came down on Brian's head. He must have had a thick skull because I took it out, he had a cry, and then we carried on playing!

Now Mrs Kirkpatrick was something else. A big, generous, warmhearted Irish woman. She lived next door at 31 and had a daughter called Irene, a little younger than me—a bit like Violet Elizabeth Bott, Just William's nemesis—and always wanted to play with the boys. This was OK as she often showed us things that boys liked to see. Also, Mrs Kirkpatrick was a Dick Barton aficionado so regularly at 6.45 p.m.; every weekday evening, the Devil's Gallop could be heard, blaring out from 31 with Jock, Snowy, and Dick up to their usual derring-do. I don't know why I did not listen to it at home. The attraction, apart from Dick was tea and a cake while we sat enthralled, knowing Dick Barton, Special Agent would always come good in the end.

Learning to Ride a Bike

Sycamore Avenue was our racetrack. Whether it was on discarded pram wheels with a plywood 'seat' or a two-wheeled homemade cart or even a prized pair of skates with metal wheels and shiny ball-bearings. But the most sought after modus operandi was a proper two-wheeled bike, preferably an adult one. At the tender age of seven in 1944, my Mam's Hercules bike was free at weekends, so my brother would volunteer to hold the saddle while I struggled for balance. After numerous fallings off, skinned knees, and dented confidence, I climbed onto the peddles—being too small to reach the saddle—and rode off with my minder. Halfway along the street,

I increased speed and, to my horror, realised I had no minder. For about 20 yards, I wobbled perilously close to the bike parting company, but for the next 100 sailed along basking in heady feelings of success before braking just before the main Hillheads road and disaster!

Mam's Granny a Mrs. MacDonald Granny Tearse's mother—
a doughty Scottish lady. About 1890.

Dad's father who I never met in 1918. A 1st W.W. medic renown for his skill with bone fractures.

Chapter 2

Whitley Bay & North Shields Education, 1948-1952

Cliffe Hotel (white building) above the paddling pool Whitley Bay. Our 'luxury' move from 33 Sycamore with Dad as Managing Director 1948. 'I used to climb down the cliffs on to the seaside rocks below the paddling pool when I was 11.'

Junior School Beckons at Rockcliffe

After four years at Bygate infants, I graduated to Whitley Bay's Rockcliffe Junior School at eight years of age. This involved taking the Hunters or United buses or 'unknitted' (as I called them before I could read properly) from Hillheads to Whitley Bay bus station a journey of about two miles costing 2d (about 1 p in decimel). From there, I had a half mile walk along Front Street to school—no 4 × 4 lifts in 1945! Along the way was Duggins bakery, and although the shop opened at 9 a.m., we would go round the back and buy a ½ p freshly baked roll. The aroma was delicious and intoxicating. To make the roll last, we would dig a small hole in the bottom and extract the soft inside, leaving the crusty exterior for our playtime at 10.30. I can even taste it now! We returned home for lunch, which meant a daily two-mile walk in all weathers! Happy days!

I was in the top class and eventually and fell in love with Brenda Davidson, and one day my infatuation got me into trouble. I had penned a juvenile love note to Brenda, the contents of which I am too mortified to remember. The form master's eagle eye intercepted the illicit note on its travel across the classroom and asked me if he should read it out to the class. Blushing to a crimson red and squirming with embarrassment, I pleaded that he didn't. He must have been a kindred spirit with a soft heart and amorous streak because he tore up the note with a warning. He had my undying gratitude from that day!

Serious Illness Stymies My Eleven-Plus Exam

I wasn't a bully, but I did have some heightened status within the class and school. For whatever reason, I saw myself as a protector of the less able and regularly 'sorted out' bullying behaviour on the smaller pupils. Then just before the eleven-plus exams, which would decide whether I went to the prestigious **Whitley Bay High Grammar School** or the Park Seniors Secondary Modern school (the school Dick Clemens & Ian Lefrenais attended, the creators of the Likely Lads series), I contracted whooping cough and was sidelined off school for four months, as a result. Long before antibiotics, whooping cough was potentially fatal, especially for sufferers of asthma, but not me fortunately. It was however transmittable, so contact with friends was out making me something of a leper. The symptoms are a 'whoop' cough that you can't stifle and continues until you almost cannot breathe. This is accompanied by a temperature, sweating, and severe loss of energy. Anyway being a fit little person, I eventually recovered and, after six months, sat the eleven-plus totally out of sync with the exams requirements. Being in the upper echelons of the top class at Rockcliffe, I was expected to pass. But I was still out of touch and on the day thought I had finished the paper when to my dismay, a teacher realised I had overlooked another page of questions. It was too late to up for the error and four weeks later, a letter arrived telling me I'd failed the eleven-plus. This was bad enough, but the worse thing was I had to say goodbye to Brenda Davidson as she had passed and went off to Whitley Bay High School, never to be seen again!

Park Seniors and Whitley Bay the North East's Riviera

The Park Secondary Modern School beckoned. Fortunatley it was only two minutes from the beach, one minute from Bertorelli's ice cream parlour, and thirty seconds from the Spanish City the area's only amusement park. With a Big Dipper, a magically smooth helter-skelter, and a House of Horrors to die for, equipped with original torture implements. It was the major after-school magnet in the Summer and Autumn months. Regrettably, it was pulled down a few years ago despite, a lively campaign by Mark Knoffler, a rock legend and Geordie by birth to keep it open.

Prior to my new school move, we had moved from Sycamore Avenue to the luxury of the Cliffe Hotel in Whitley Bay, which Dad and some partners had bought for £12,000 in 1948. This meant leaving my friends at Hillheads, who went to Bygate Senior School in Monkseaton. However, I spent two enjoyable years at Park School between 1948 and 1950, mainly due to my introduction to football in the school team where I was about the smallest goalkeeper in the league. I was also top of the class at metalwork and English. Ms Sweet our form mistress was, like her name, a sweetie taking us for English and R. I. (religious instruction) and spent many hours debunking all the miracles with practical and believable reasons all of which I remember today. For example, in the Water into Wine miracle, Jesus emptied water into old wine barrels which could after a while have imparted some of the wine flavour into the water. I was also good at English (reading and writing) so became a bit of favourite of Ms Sweet.

Food rationing was still in place, and I had my first taste of school meals and to this day can still smell the boiled cabbage—ugh! Mind you, we still cleared the plates!

Near to the hotel was the rocks, and on the rocks was the Rock pool about a quarter mile away, which was scoured clean by the sea at every tide. Many years previously, it had been hacked out of the rocks to about 30' square and 3' deep with a rusty grab rail and slippery wooden steps. By the age of nine, I could swim underwater but never mastered swimming on the surface until one day when I was eleven years old I saw a women swimming up and down effortlessly. I thought well if she can do it so can I, so I promptly jumped in and swam. I never did have a swimming lesson until forty years later when I was training for the Ironman triathlons.

A mile further along the coast was a delightful little fishing village Cullercoats with a small harbour, an RNLI Boathouse and marine laboratory, which stored all kinds for fish mainly from the North Sea. As it was free entry, we would spend an hour on school holidays admiring the vast selection of fish. But in warm weather, the best pastime was racing along the harbour pier and diving into the sea but only when the tide was in! The competition was seeing who could get farthest from the pier.

Years later when I was about thirty, I found an old school photo from Park Secondary Modern and met up with some who still lived in the area—including my ex-sweetheart Clare Surtees. I was living in London and married with two little ones then, so it stayed a fond memory.

Learning to swim (centre) at the Rock Pool age 10, Whitley Bay 1947. 'I saw someone swimming so I copied them' Note The Shipwrecked Greek Freighter—Our Playground At Low Tide!'

Slaughter at the Cliffe Hotel

After the war, Dad became the personnel manager at Beck's Shoe Polish factory, which had been producing munitions during the war while Dad had been a government inspector. He didn't get on with the owner, who was a dictatorial tyrant, and eventually left to buy his own hotel in Whitley Bay with the help of a business consortium. The year was 1948, and rationing was still in place, but Dad had some excellent farmers and food suppliers, who could circumvent the regulations to supply the Cliffe Hotel. Gradually the business built up with astute marketing and professional management by encouraging specialist groups and conferences to offset the winter decline in tourist business. The Post Office I remember had regular training weekends, and for recreation, they turned the dining room into a games area after dinner. At eleven years old, I was sports mad and quickly became a dab hand at table tennis with adult tuition, thanks to the post office.

In the hotel car park, the maintenance staff had helped me build a pigeon ducket (loft), and after a few months, I had collected a flock of a dozen pedigree pigeons. Some of these had been 'attracted' by sending my pigeons up when there were races in the region. Tired or disoriented pigeons would be nursed down by my group for food and rest. After a few weeks, they became part of my group, and many mated and hatched 'squeakers' to swell the numbers.

On one occasion, a jet black ringed racing pigeon was lured down by my flock—very unusual and a type unknown to me. Unfortunately, this beautiful bird heralded the most heartbreaking event of my young life. Seven days after the black pigeon's arrival, I went to feed my flock and, on opening the ducket's door, was faced with a scene of utter devastation! Of my twenty-one birds, only six were still alive. The remainder were either dead or dying—their throats or breasts ripped out. I was completely shocked by what seemed an unbelievable sight. The beautiful birds I had reared, developed, and trained were no more. The carnage was almost complete. I was eleven years old then, and even now when I recall the scene, I am filled with remorse. Perhaps I could have prevented it with better security. Almost in a zombie-like state, I took out the dead birds and those beyond hope put out of their misery. I released the six still alive and terrorised to find a better home as they would never return to my ducket again. I was still in a daze when I told my mam and dad who were also totally shocked, as they knew how much the flock meant to me. Who was the culprit and what had gone on a killing spree? I never knew for certain, but by all accounts, it was a large rat that had squeezed in, in search of food and ended my dreams of pigeon racing. After that I never owned another pigeon!

Young Ladies Enter Dale's Life

Living at the Cliffe Hotel was in other ways idyllic. Walls ice cream on tap—the unique flavour is still the same now as it was then. I was a minute or two from the sea, rocks, and the Rock Pool where I learned to swim with no tuition! Whitley Bay sands were three minutes away, and, of course, there was always the Spanish City. Young female visitors to the hotel with their families in summer time were also in abundance. Despite my tender years, I fell in love regularly and, on more than one occasion, shinned up a drainpipe to the first floor to serenade and smooch with a young lady from Jesmond, who always reminded me of Moira Shearer (no relation to Alan) the star of the film *Red Shoes*. These amorous encounters usually lasted a week or two, depending on their length of stay.

Next door to the hotel was a family with two youngsters who required a regular babysitter. Who better than the Hotel Managing Director's son! I didn't have far to go, and the money was an ideal addition to my paper-round income. I recall the amount of two shillings (20 p) as the nightly remuneration which in those days in 1949 had the buying power of about £2 at today's prices. My paper round didn't last though as I could not get the hang of matching up the papers with the addresses. Also Dad did not think it appropriate for a Hotel Director's son to have to descend to the level of a newspaper boy! What a humbug!

After the pigeon episode, I was given a Heinz variety collie puppy by the name of Blimp (after the Colonel's WW1 fame), and for a year, it was a great companion. Unfortunately, it developed a nasty habit of chasing motor cars and resting, usually in the middle of the road, which it did once too often. Shortly after, a substitute arrived in the shape of Mike, a golden cross retriever. It was actually my sister's and her new husband John Flint, but as they were often away from the hotel, I was granted regular ownership. I still have a photo of me and Mike outside the hotel with one of the chambermaids Maisie, who also had a lovely daughter whom I do remember fondly.

I begin to learn about the concept of financial motivation

My move from Sycamore Avenue to the Cliff Hotel meant that I then had access to a piano, the previous council house being too small. Dad appointed a piano teacher Ms Money who took me up to Grade 1 in the Associate Board exam with pieces that stretched my little fingers to breaking point. Being twelve years old, I'd rather have played with friends or raced pigeons or chased young ladies, but Dad insisted I practise. Eventually, his cunning ploy to get me to practise was to dangle a very tasty carrot that he knew would be irresistible. That was 'pass your Grade 1 exam, and I'll buy you a new bike'. That was some carrot because bikes then cost somewhere in the region of about three years pocket money—that is £12 plus! Anyway within weeks, I had worn my tiny fingers down and stretched them to a full octave to play Mozart's Einer Kleiner Nacht Musiche or at least the first part and duly scraped through the exam. Next, I was down to Lavery's bike shop in Cullercoats to check out the options. Yes, £12 would buy a rather tasty Hercules bike which would be the envy of my peer group. Back to Dad: 'Oh well,' he said, 'I didn't mean to buy you a bike immediately'. *What!* I screamed and danced up and down and accused him of lying to me and being untrustworthy and lots of other nasty accusations. My ire was well and truly up. Next, I convinced my Mam who was in the picture of what had been promised. She might be small and unassuming, but in matters of honour, she was a terrier and put Dad well and truly to the sword. Shortly after, I had my £12 and a sparkling Hercules 3 speed bicycle!

An Unhappy Relocation—Again!

Just when my life was settled with local friends and Park Seniors Secondary Modern where I had a girlfriend, Claire Surtees, was a fully functioning member of the senior football team in goal and coming top in English and Metalwork, 'disaster' struck again. Dad had made an unqualified success of the Cliff Hotel after two years and had plans to develop more rooms but then had a very public argument with one of the company directors. Although I never really knew the full story, it appears this director was worse for wear and insulted my Mam. Dad was not the forgiving type, and he did have a rather short fuse at times. Unfortunately, the director was a major shareholder and left Dad no option but to resign.

So in short, we all packed up and moved to a relative 'slum' in North Shields some three miles away in Albion Road opposite St. Mary's church.

Dad's new business had been a cafe of sorts which he renamed Cafe Concord. Meals were served during the day in a fifteen-seat dining room behind a bar counter, serving drinks and snacks. Dad did the cooking initially and Mam waited on. Our accommodation at the rear could be best described as basic with one lounge/dining room, a scullery downstairs, and one large room upstairs, split into two by wardrobes and a temporary curtain to make two bedrooms, one for me and my brother and one for Mam and Dad. Thinking back it was such a come-down after the hotel that I could not imagine how Dad had made such a rash and ill-conceived decision. In addition to the Cafe, there were some limited opportunities for outside catering, which included the local Masonic Hall as Dad had become a Mason.

Holiday Camps and Testerone Rising

While at the Albion Road, I went on a number of school youth camps and joined first the Sea Scounts—not enough sailing, then the Army Cadets—couldn't get to play the bugle and finally the Boys Brigade, who met in a large room above the Cafe. On one camp in the Cheviots, our leader decided to climb Mount Cheviot and had not done his homework regarding distance, height of climb, and provisions for fourteen-year-olds. Eventually we reached the summit with a bar of chocolate between ten and eventually returned, completed exhausted and starving hungry. Our dinner that evening is etched on my mind forever. We opened just about every tin in the camp into a saucepan, heated it up, and devoured it to the last drop. Heinz Tomato Soup tins in the supermarkets bring back this memory into stark relief.

On another school camp, one of our more forward pupils and schoolfried Eddy Southworth, a butcher's son, decided one day to demonstrate his new-found pleasure activity. As we gathered around, he removed his shorts and proceeded to masturbate himself vigorously to a climax. The outcome was a complete shock and revelation to most of us, but it wasn't long before we decided to copy. Back at Albion Road my later discovery of Dad's *Health and Efficiency* magazines were a great help to me in that respect, yet I never found out if he had missed them! Eddy also introduced me to the new technology of the era—T.V. In 1953, he invited a select few from the class to his house to see the status symbol of the whole school a 14' black-and-white television with one channel. His Dad's butchers must have been very successful in those days. Later I returned to North Shields when I was at the Connaught Hotel and found Eddy successfully in charge of the butcher shop.

Stuck at a Secondary Modern Boys School

Grand plans of sending me to a private school in Tynemouth evaporated as the finances dwindled, and, horror of horrors, I had to leave Park Seniors for the down-market squalor of Linskill Boys School a quarter mile from the cafe. I was now thirteen years old, still in short pants as everyone else and attached to the 'A' class. Memories of my two years there are not particularly enjoyable, although I tended to make the best of situations. The girls' school was adjacent and severely off limits.

Discarding the goalkeepers jersey I made the first team, Linskill 'A' at centre-forward and scored regularly, but do not recall winning anything. We did not play rugby, cricket, or even athletics, these sports being the province of Tynemouth High Grammar School, even though it was in the centre of North Shields. The only time we had cross country running was given as a punishment by the P.E. master in lieu of playing football! There was occasional swimming in the open-air pool on Tynemouth sands, and again like the Rock Pool, it was filled with sea water and usually freezing! During the summer, it was occasionally warm and the art deco-styled pool has fountains and springboards and high diving boards from which we did dares. My party piece was a handstand from the top board and 1½ sumersaults off the spring board. Today's health and safety culture would have been appalled at the danger, and although there were a few accidents, it was all part of growing up. Years later, I returned to Tynemouth and found the pool and surrounds closed and in an advanced state of decay with the pool itself filled with gigantic rocks. What a waste! It could have been heated and updated. Instead they spent more local funds on a new indoor pool in Preston Village about three miles away and another indoor wave pool in Whitley Bay. My bedroom wall still sports a British Rail publicity poster of Tynemouth in the 30's showing the open air pool in all its splendour!

Linskill 'A' football team with Mr. Lee form master. I'm second left bottom row. Notice we're all wearing different socks, two different shirts and our goalkeeper is the SMALLEST in the team! Team kit funds were very tight! 1952.

Nurse Cherry (Mary) Lyons training at
Guys Hospital London my elder sister (by 8 years) 1951.

No Homework or Career Expectations

At school, we were never given homework, nor did we cover biology, languages, physics, or drama; in fact very little culture or higher learning at all. Being a secondary modern school, the assumption was our occupational horizon was set well below the professions and perhaps just above the labouring classes. Job expectations would relate to mining, engineering, shipbuilding, police, and possibly clerical, although I do not recall ever getting any career advice. However, being in the A stream and near the top of the class in most academic and practical subjects, I was given the opportunity along with another pupil of sitting the thirteen-plus examination. This was a sort of second bite of the Grammar school cherry but like the eleven plus, I failed that too. The one highlight I recall in my entire time there was achieving second prize in the school chess championships to Arthur Shipley—I won the first game, stale-mated the second, and getting carried away lost the next two in the best of three final. I was also presented with a Certificate for Proficiency in Senior Football but no qualifications!

My goal on leaving school was to become a newspaper reporter, but first I had to get some appropriate skills such as shorthand and typing! Cue the Pitmans Commercial College (North Shields branch) with typing and shorthand.

Chapter 3

Early Jobs & Leaving For London, 1953-1958

Pitmans College North Shields

Whenever I hear a piece of classical music on Classic FM, I am transported back immediately to a repetitive typing exercise at Pitmans College. We had to type at different speeds set by a 78 rpm record with each beat a letter. As we improved—15 in a class—the record was speeded up. I studied at the college for twelve months after leaving Linskill School at fifteen and passed two typing, (35 & 45 wpm) and two shorthand exams, (60 & 80 wpm). My desire to become a news reporter led me to write applications to every paper in the area but no takers, even as a tea boy. Bearing in mind that my Dad was very friendly with an editor on the Newcastle Journal and my brother-in-law John Flint was the sub-editor on the Seaside Chronicle in Whitley Bay, none of these contacts helped get me into the news world. This left me with the suspicion that Dad was determined to have me follow in his catering footsteps. I've never really forgiven him for overlooking my real career interests at the time. But then why did he pay for me to learn shorthand and typing?

My First Paid Job—Tyne Furniture Works—Clerk Typist

Eventually all my job applications paid off with an offer at the Tyne Furniture Works (TFW) on the Coast Road Estate, a fifteen minute bus ride from the cafe. I became a clerk/typist in the goods inwards accounts department, and apart from clerical duties, I sometimes used my shorthand for the occasional letter. TFW was part of GUS (Great Universal Stores) and produced mainly utility bedroom furniture with attractive names such as the Balham, Peckham, and Brixton Suites, names of South London suburbs that at the time had little meaning for me. However, I can still recall walking through the works being jeered at as an 'office toff' by the assembly workers and the overpowering, Pervasive smell of wood glue.

I had worked there only four months when a personal disaster struck. Returning one night from the Howard, a local cinema after seeing John Wayne crush the Japanese again, I felt light-headed and disoriented. The next morning I was sweating and delirious. The doctor was called, and he quickly diagnosed pneumonia and pleurisy. This was at a time before antibiotics, when influenza and other nasties like mumps and chickenpox posed serious and often terminal health risks. For the two weeks I was comatose all I recall, drifting in and out of consciousness, was vague shapes of people coming and going. Being a tough little soul, I eventually recovered but was unable to return to my job for six whole months! Once I had recovered 100 % Mam told me that for a period it was touch and go so obviously God thought I was too good to go. However, for six months regular as clockwork, the TFW posted me my weekly wage of thirty-five shillings (£1.75p). What company these days would be so generous to a new employee? Once I returned to the TFW boredom quickly set in as I could not see my future nailed to an office desk—I wanted more action!

Tilley's Restaurant—My Apprenticeship Starts—1953

I was just not cut out for an office job, especially one far removed from any newspaper link, so once I had recovered, my Dad, realising my lack of interest in slaving over a typewriter, suggested a catering apprenticeship. Loath that I was to abandon my desire to be an ace reporter, I agreed to give it a try. Dad had worked for Tilley's in Grey Street Newcastle many years before as a waiter on outside-catering jobs. These often involved catering on ships undergoing sea trials from the Tyne before they were commissioned, and could be liners, freighters, or fighting ships. It was very good money in the 1930s and not really hard work serving a few officers and technicians. One day early in his experience at sea, he asked where the dirty plates and cutlery were washed up. 'Oh just stick 'em in Davy Jones locker, mate' was the reply. In other words, dump them out the porthole!

There was apparently more than enough crockery and cutlery to last out the trip, even with this cavalier approach to the crockery.

At Tilley's Restaurant ostensibly the 'best' restaurant in Newcastle, I was an apprentice under the Hotel & Catering Institute scheme. Initially, for the five year apprenticeship I was on a level with a KP's (kitchen porter) status. The one blessing was we didn't work evenings, although that is when the real skills were learnt and demonstrated. My eighteenth months at Tilley's taught me how to handcut and fry chips. Wow! Each day I would slice potatoes into 3" × ½" chips into a water-filled dustbin. When filled to the brim, I would than blanch (cook without colouring) these into a deep fat fryer to be ready at lunch time when they were flash fried until crisp and brown. I would then crack four trays of eggs (120) into a large stainless receptacle and beat then up ready for the chef d'omlette. Not much of that eighteen months is memorable except for a few exceptions. Once I had mastered omelette making, I did graduate for a time, to the upstairs restaurant service area where I would receive the meals from the basement kitchen and serve them to the waitresses. On one occasion, there were shrieks from the restaurant as a result of a rather large rat running along the skirting in the dining area! Large rats were commonplace in the basement stores where the night watchman would reduce the numbers with the aid of pistol, but only marginally.

Diversions in the Kitchen at Tilley's

Another interesting diversion and aid to my sex education took place in the pastry section where the young debonair patissier regularly took enormous liberties with his female assistant often in full view of the apprentices. As the only female in the kitchen, she seemed unfazed with these liberties and seemed to enjoy the attention. These sessions occurred mainly in the après lunch periods, when the chefs had left.

Our KP (kitchen porter) was also a colourful character. KPs as a breed are usually failed citizens whose only requirements are food, an undemanding job and enough money to render themselves blotto every pay-day evening. Joe was a Canadian and tunesmith and knew and sang many of the old music hall songs ad nauseum. Three I particularly remember were 'Any Old Iron' later a hit of Peter Sellers, 'Pale Hands I'll Hold Beside the Shalimar' apparently a romantic and evocative river in India and 'My little Wooden Hut' (I wouldn't leave for you).

In addition, I attended a rather basic FE College in Benton a Newcastle suburb to learn the rudiments of cookery theory on a day release basis. Most of the other students were from 'inferior' industrial establishments which in my ignorance I felt superior to. My sole memory of this tuition was the domestic science approach of both the establishment and the training. I do however remember making a delightful bread pudding.

My one non-catering skill I learnt in Newcastle was to ballroom dance at a 'Studio Dance Class' in Walker, two miles from the restaurant. With me went the Ainsley twins, two other apprentices. This stood me in good stead when I eventually transferred my apprenticeship to a prestigious Mayfair hotel in London.

An Apprenticeship and Move to London's Connaught Hotel

Dad decided that Tilley's did not have the top status it once commanded in the restaurant business, and his focus turned to London's quality hotels. Tilley's did not cut the mustard for my Dad who had worked in many of London's top hotels in the 1930s. Whether he selected the Connaught or whether it was chosen by the Hotel & Catering Institute I never knew. But certainly it was the magnet for royalty, stars of stage, screen, media, and top politicians, all of whom expected quality and discretion above all. Price was no barrier to these fortunate few. The Connaught Hotel in South Audley Street in the heart of Mayfair was a small unassuming hotel with only seventy rooms and apartments but with a regal ambiance, a Michelin rated restaurant and grillroom to die for. However, in 1954, you could still get a three course table d'hote luncheon for only 17/6 (75 p)!

It was without doubt London's piece de resistance in the hotel business and certainly not to be confused with the Connaught Rooms, a very large banqueting centre—which it often was. My first job at the Connaught was in the patisserie under the Master Patissier Wally Ladd and 1st Commis Roger Taylor, the only all English section in the kitchen. The executive chef was a dapper little Frenchman called Pierre Emile Toulemon not unlike Hercule Poiret in stature, demeanour, and appearance. He had been an apprentice at the George V hotel in Paris under the tutelage of the renowned chef Escoffier, creator of the menu format and author of the seminal work of cuisine garnishes the Repetoire de la Cuisine. So, I can justifiably claim to be Escoffier's apprentice's apprentice! My wage in 1954 was £1.17.6 (£1.87 p) boosted to £3.00 just before I left for H. M. National Service four years later!

Many years later, I returned to the Connaught but as a customer, this time through the front door, and imagine my surprise when I realised the menus were almost identical in style and content to when I was an apprentice forty-five years earlier. Only the prices had been changed!

The Connaught kitchen was in the basement, worked by about fifteen chefs and other staff (no women), the vast majority of whom were continental, that is German, French, Swiss, and Belgian. This kitchen was very small by contrast to most luxury hotels but with an enviable reputation and clientele. The language used in the kitchen was French; that is all menu orders and responses were in French. Imagine a young Geordie with a local north-east dialect wrestling with French dishes and garnishes—a daunting task but one which was a constant source of amusement to the kitchen brigade.

What I do remember of the Connaught experience was for two years, I boarded at the John Benn (Boys) Hostel in Stockwell Road, Brixton S. E. London. After which I moved to B & B's in various parts of London with a pal from the hostel Pat Langmead, who became a foreign office civil servant.

The Connaught Hotel's staff Christmas party at the Kensington Town Hall with the pastry chefs brigade. From L. Wally Ladd (deceased) Head Pattisier. Me at 18; Roger Taylor 1st commis and seated Jean Dick a top Belgium chocolatier and rake on transfer. 1956.

Leisure and Education Pursuits at the Connaught

I rarely had a weekend or public holidays off as they were reserved for the chef du parties (section heads) so bang went my football career to eventually play for Newcastle United. However, a popular kitchen perk was two free pints of beer daily brought to us by the KP, apparently to offset dehydration caused by working in high temperatures. Working mainly in the patisserie and often on day shifts, the kitchen climate was fine. Occasionally when obliged for my training to work in the main kitchen or larder, I worked split shifts 9-2 p.m. and 5-9 p.m. This effectively ruined your day as your time off was effectively reduced to two hours after changing and preparation for the evening. Many chefs spent this time in the dressing room playing cards for money. The favourite game—the only game I recall—was 'Nap' which was a form of five card whist where one player makes a bid up to five hands and the others try to stop him often for money. Usually I would play if the weather was poor but in the summer I'd go to Hyde Park, five minutes away to swim in the serpentine or sunbathe.

As part of the apprenticeship, I went on day release for City & Guilds qualifications 150 and 151 catering initially at Westminster Technical College, which was then tops for the full time students but bottom for day-release apprentices. The Principal, Mr Vincent (Old Two Thousand as he was called by students, i.e. vingt cent), did not approve of City & Guilds or part-time students so I decided to transfer my allegiance to the Borough Polytechnic in Southwark. After passing both courses, I enrolled on a Continental Confectioner Course in the final year which involved making, among other things, liquor chocolates—a skill I retain to this day to my daughters and family's delight.

Mam & Dad at the Tower of London visiting me
when at the Connaught. 1956.

Catering for the Cognocenti at the Connaught

Three memorable events happened while working weekends. One Sunday morning in the Mews on my way to work, I recognised a familiar figure approaching. It turned out to be the famous American actor Rod Steiger who starred in a number of hit films *On The Waterfront with Marlon Brando, Twelve Angry Men,* and the musical *Oklahoma.* As he passed, I called 'Good morning, Mr Steiger' to which he responded with a cheery wave. The same afternoon, I was briefly on my own when a waiter called at the serving hatch and ordered a poire dame blanche dessert and then said 'make it special it's for Princess Grace (of Monaco)'. On another weekend lunchtime, a waiter friend called at the hatch 'come quick there's someone you want to see in the Grillroom'. I dashed up the stairs and peeped through the service doors to see another famous American film actor and a particular favourite of mine—Richard Widmark. My day was made. I was also told that the great screen actress Katherine Hebburn had an apartment at the hotel. The Connaught in fact was a popular haunt for the rich and famous but who required privacy above all and tucked away in the centre of Mayfair it was the embodiment of discretion. Being in Mayfair, I would routinely get a buzz at seeing famous celebrities on the streets.

Learning Patisserie Specialities

In the patisserie, we made all our own ice creams, chocolates, cakes and petit fours, and Christmas puddings (always a year in advance). On regular basis, we imported specialists from Swiss and Belgium patisseries to exchange ideas and techniques on all things patisserie. And, when things were slow at weekends and evenings, the commis and apprentices would experiment with sugar-work flowers and blown fruit—quite hazardous if you sucked! We also made models in pastillage, a mouldable mixture of icing sugar and gum tragazanth, and in the Hotel & Catering Exhibition at Olympia in 1958, I made a model of the new bridge in St. James' Park for which I was awarded an honourable mention and certificate. I had hoped for a gold medal but had to admit it wasn't up to a winner's standard. My best time in the pastry department was to work a straight shift 9 a.m. through to 5 p.m. On those days, my job would be to prepare all the petit fours and the dessert trolley for the evening service. This allowed me to develop my creativity with designs on the Mille Fuille (Vanilla Cream Slices) and making peppermint humbugs out of pulled sugar. After which I would do a deal with Wally, the breakfast cook, by swapping pastries for steaks (usually filet) and have my 'evening' meal before I left for Brixton on my seven mile return bike ride to Stockwell and the Hostel.

My London Accommodation at the John Benn Hostel

At the hostel, I was charged the enormous sum of £1.15.0 (£1.75 p) for my weekly accommodation, including meals at weekends. In other words, I had 2/6 (12.5 p) 'spending' money. Surprisingly, I did actually save something and bought a bike and later on a Dansett record player for my EP/ LP records. What luxury! My first EP was the Dave Brubeck Quartet with Frenesi, which I played continuously and still have today. In 1955, the Boy's Club movement was in full swing having been sponsored by stars such as Frankie Vaughan the 1950s heart-throb. At this time, the conquest of Everest and the sub-four-minute mile record occurred in the same year as the opening of the Brixton Boy's Club, which featured some 'A' list personnel. The opening ceremony included youngsters from clubs in the area and included John Benn resident Dale Robinson Lyons no less. This ceremony was also broadcasted live on BBC TV (there was only one TV station then!). Naturally the Lyons' clan and others were glued to sets in faraway Tyneside to see their 'little' boy of eighteen performing in front of the ikons of the day Roger Bannister and the Duke of Edinburgh. Dale was lucky enough to get a photo with himself and the celebrities. This photo taken fifty-six years ago still has pride of place on my sideboard and is a great conversation piece!

Me (topless) winning the obstacle race age 18 with, from left Roger Bannister 1st 4 minute miler & the Duke of Edinburgh at Brixton Boys Club opening. Shown live on BBC TV (the only TV station) & watched by the family & neighbours. 1955.

Deaths in the Family

Shortly after, Granny Tearse, who had been living on her own in Northumberland Street became increasingly frail and was often found wandering the streets, died at the age of eighty-four. She was the only grandparent I ever knew; the others had died or disappeared before I was born. She was a stoic and stout Salvationist—I still have her photo in bonnet and uniform. She was buried in Preston Cemetery. Almost one year later, I received an urgent call at the Connaught to go home immediately. I arrived at Exeter Road to be told that Mam was seriously ill with little hope of recovery. On my previous visit to home, Mam had not been well and was apparently receiving treatment for what I later learnt was cervical cancer. In those days, the big 'C' was never talked about so I was totally ignorant of her real condition until two days before she died. She was nursed at home by Cherry, my sister, and I remember holding Mam's hand the day before hoping for a miracle. The doctor arrived that day and, when the family had assembled, told us there was no hope. The next afternoon, Cherry went upstairs, and I heard her cry out 'Mam, Mam, Oh Mam'! I couldn't bear to go upstairs after she came and told us Mam had died. I took Sam the dog out and walked for hours, trying to blot out the sight of Mam lying dead. She was only fifty-three, and I often think that had she had the same cancer today, she would probably have survived. Dad never really recovered from losing someone that had been his partner and wife for thirty years. Through all the war years, trials of his business problems and successes, and losing his leg, she had been there for him and for all of us. A model mother and wife Mary Josephine Lyons nee Tearse R. I. P. Mam was buried in Preston Cemetery in July 1955 near to Granny Tearse.

Mam relaxing on the Dunes at Seaton Sluice.
near Whitley Bay about 12 months before she died. 1952.

Deferred National Service and a French Transfer Thwarted

National Service called during 1955 also, but fortunately I was deferred until my apprenticeship was completed at the Connaught. A year later, I attempted to transfer to Southern France for a six months chefs development programme, but the National Service board refused my application on the grounds I might flee the country to avoid conscription—unbelievable! I was later to get some measure of revenge on my National Service masters.

My days off were always during the week, and one stop from Stockwell tube station was the Oval cricket ground. At the time, Australia was playing Surrey at Kennington Oval with the ace Bedser twin bowlers, Alex & Eric. They proceeded to skittle out the Aussies between them to win the match. Alec took all ten Aussie wickets in the second innings for a new and still unbroken record. Riveted by this good fortune, I sat on a wooden bench all day, and on returning to Stockwell Road, my back seized up. And although I was only nineteen was shuffling along like an eighty-year old. To my shame, an elderly lady took my arm asking if I needed some help—crossing the road!

Moving up the Accommodation Ladder

Shortly after my second bike was stolen from the hostel, I decided to find my own accommodation. With my pal Pat Langmead, we moved into bedsit-land. First stop was in Kennington, SE London, then after a short stay near the BBC HQ's at Shepherds Bush, West London, and then a 'luxury' pad in Earls Court's Pennywern Road. Unfortunately, we were summarily expelled from there for fiddling the gas meter but not before I lost my virginity! Pat was on holiday when I invited a young lady from Turnham Green to the bedsit. She obviously had more experience than me, regarding sexual relations and quickly got down to business. There may have been relief and a slightly damaged sense of achievement, but it was not a success, and I never saw her again.

Finally, Pat and I returned to Victoria SE1 with Mrs Connelly, a buxom Irish lady, first with a tiny bedsitter with a double bed and gas ring at £2.00 weekly and then finally in a lovely double room with gas ring, overlooking St. Georges Square for £2.17.6d. (£2.87 p). We were on the up! Mrs Connelly became a surrogate mother to us and would regularly invite us for tea when we went to pay the rent. When Pat eventually got called up for National Service at eighteen, I left Mrs Connelly's tender care and ended up in a flat in the next street, recommended by a friend of my new girlfriend Angela Valentine (later to become Mrs Lyons).

I Meet My Future Wife

Working most weekends at the Connaught rather stifled my opportunities to meet the fair sex, but on one occasion, I went dancing at the Kensington Town Hall—live bands were in vogue then but now a thing of the past in most places. However, I noticed two young ladies, one of whom looked quite tasty, so I put my training to the test and invited her on to the floor for a quickstep. She was quite a good mover, neatly turned out, slim, short-bobbed auburn hair, and green eyes and danced very close! Anyway a few dances later, there seemed to be some chemistry. I got chatting to her girl-friend and found they also lived in Victoria, round the corner from my bedsit. Towards the end of the evening after a few beers to bolster my courage, I asked for her phone number and got it. She was an eighteen year old secretary and didn't seem to mind that I was an apprentice chef albeit in a prestigious hotel so after a few dates, she became my regular girl back in 1957. A year later, I was in the RAF and, two years later, married to Angela Valentine at St. Nicholas Church in Rochester Row. But, more about that later.

As I was paid so little, I took a dishwasher's job at the Cumberland Hotel near Marble Arch and lasted one whole day! The dishwashing area was in the bowels of the hotel, steamy hot, dimly lit with a mechanised dish conveyor belt, so you had to keep up. Drinking water was from a communal trough with tin cups chained to the side. I do not remember speaking to anyone during that time nor do I remember getting paid either.

I also applied for a transfer to Claridges Hotel where I thought I might learn more and more importantly get paid more. The reply was in the negative as I was indentured to the Connaught but I later discovered a transfer could have been arranged, had the personnel manager, Mr Bell, been more amenable. The kind Mr Bell then informed me I would be better if my day release to the Borough Poly was taken from my time off. This meant that during term time, I had one day off not two. As I was also taking evening classes, I decided to take two half days off instead, so I could still attend French classes. In effect, I was working every day at the Connaught for fifty weeks a year. One wonders why the hotel trade has recruitment problems! Despite all the problems, long hours, split shifts, low wages, I did eventually become a skilled patissier and to a lesser degree a qualified Master Chef.

Final Days of the Apprentice Chef

After four years, I eventually received my signed indentures having completed a satisfactory apprenticeship. In all the time at the Connaught, not once was I given any planned training, written training plans, or progress evaluation of any systematic kind. Nor was there any formal agreement specifying what I would learn or where I would be trained in the kitchen or for how long. In fact, I was a cheap labour source to learn from watching and doing. Little interest was taken in my studies at Borough. In fact, the usual response if I questioned anything or attempted to use recipes or suggest things I had learned was 'practice not theory is the way to learn' from the chefs du parties! A pretty damning indictment of the Hotel & Catering Institute, the apprenticeship system at that time, and in a wider context the industry, in general! Little wonder, the labour turnover of hotel staff is so high.

I did learn a great deal, however, both at the hotel and at college and made some long-lasting male friends—another Geordie, who worked at the Grosvenor House Hotel on Park Lane. After I returned from the States in 1965, I bumped into my Geordie friend who had opened a new venture with support from Billy Walker, the British heavyweight champion at the time, called Billy's Baked Potato, the first baked potato outlet in the UK! Some of the chefs from the Connaught were kept in touch and in fact I still have contact with my pastry chef 'boss' Roger Taylor whom I met again at the College of Food in Birmingham years later.

More about the 'College of Grub & Scrub' later! But, after four years in the kitchens, the Government came calling in the guise of the National Service commissioners. I decided to serve in Her Majesty's Royal Air Force for two years—an honour I was really looking forward to.

Chapter 4

National Service in the Royal Air Force, 1958-1961

Basic Training in Wilmslow Cheshire

There was no party for me when I left the Connaught. I would have been surprised if there had been considering the penurious attitude to staff and benefits. My RAF call came prior to the end of my apprenticeship at the age of twenty in January 1958. After a short break in North Shields, I headed South to six-weeks basic training at RAF Wilmslow in Cheshire a centre where I was kitted out and received my first stripe—compliments of my apprenticeship and City & Guilds examinations—to Junior Technician. What status I had when enjoying the envious stares of the other RAF novices. Apart from square bashing and peeling potatoes, getting up at 6 a.m. in freezing billets with twenty mostly homesick airmen, and hearing the NCO's balling out 'alright you 'orrible airmen, hands off cxxxs and on with socks,' the period was uneventful. The first NCO joker called us together and asked who wanted to be a pilot. A number of hands went up but not mine. 'OK,' he said, calling the gullible few forward, 'See that pile of rubbish outside the kitchens. Well, go and pile it in that skip over there!' Ha! Ha! We were also given rifle drill and training with an ancient Enfield 307, but despite that I was awarded a marksman badge and allocated another 1 shilling (5 p) a day extra to my ten shillings (50 p) weekly pay. J/T 3153376 Lyons was on his way. As part of our acclimatisation, we were crowded into a blockhouse where a canister of tear gas was released—the first to 'escape' from the room, eyes streaming, was given a dressing down by the NCO for being a wimp! One trick that was played on a vulnerable sleeping recruit by the sadists in the billet was during the night, they would gently place the trainee's hand in a pail of very cold water. The shock would often result in their waking rather rudely, realising they had wet the bed! Very naughty but highly amusing to some!

Another Type of Cookery at RAF Halton

At the end of our sixteen weeks basic training, we were granted a week off, and I returned to North Shields To Dad's home cooking and bought my first motorbike, a 1937 Francis Barnet for £18. What a bargain! Although quite reliable its top speed was only 45 mph but happier doing about 35 mph, so my journey to my chef's training camp at Halton near Aylesbury took about nine hours and two breakdowns! This sixteen week cookery training was to acclimatise us to the real world of cooking for the military in situations far removed from the cosy environment of civvy street and the Connaught's luxury. We were taught to cook food where no stoves existed. Techniques for cooking in the dessert in straw boxes buried in the sand to maintain sufficient heat to cook—very economical. It was all new to me, but my good basic training helped to get me through with some commendation. The training sergeants had other strings to their bow in the form of Hunt Balls, Wedding Receptions, and Outside Catering for which they were well equipped both in knowledge and equipment. I recall helping out on one particular Hunt Ball in the area where the buffet was an amazing spread of the most expensive kind. Lobsters, whole salmon, smoked salmon, whole hams, caviar, in fact a veritable cornucopia of quality. Naturally we were paid separately for these off site 'gigs' and had for ourselves the most tasty leftovers!

Headquarters Bomber Command—Nap Hill—Officers' Mess

Towards the end of the training, I received my permanent posting to exotic High Wycombe at a place called Nap Hill—top secret HQ of Bomber Command with a complement of 400 on the base. I would be working in the officers' mess kitchens so the catering should be more of a challenge than the OR's (other ranks) mess. Having catering qualifications, I was then selected to become the reserve chef for the C in C's (Commander in Chief) residence when he was away. I would have to cook for his wife and household staff in the main. This terrified me at the time, yet it was an easy option, involving the most basic meals. In addition, I was also selected for the Command Catering Team (CCT). This meant flying to other RAF stations to cater for visiting VIP's such as Princess Margaret, and because of this high status post, the CCT did no parades, and I had every other weekend off. What bliss!

I was also able to resume my soccer career and was selected for the command football team—no easy feat as some of the team were playing for league clubs at the weekend—on the understanding that they would play for us during the week. Barry Sluman and Charlie Nicholas played for Chelsea's first team so gave us enough skill and ability to help us win the RAF's FA Cup in 1960 at Uxbridge Stadium. I came close to scoring in the first minute but our 2-0 score line against the favourites was more than compensation. The winner's medal was about 1" diameter which I kept enshrined in a plastic dome for decades—but alas no longer. During that time, I also played for a High Wycombe team on a Saturday and remember one game we won by a hatful, and as an inside forward I scored 5, one of which I knocked from the goalkeepers hands (a move now outlawed).

Corporal Technician Lyons (centre) + two cooks at
RAF Bomber Command Officers Mess. Nap Hill,
High Wycombe. Age 23. 1960 A National Service
conscript on 10 shillings (50p) weekly.

Sking the moguls in Tigne, France, Haute Savoire—1983

Dick & Dale resting after a hard days skiing. Flaine, Haute Savoire France—2002

We had great fun in the officers' mess with my National Service pals, one of which had RAF as his initials—Robin A Flynn. He was about 6'3' and became a catering manager for the American Air Force base in High Wycombe I visited the base to see a staggering variety of ultra modern items of catering equipment, techniques, and products, none of which had made their way to UK in 1961. Everything including steaks and ice cream was imported from the States. I always remember his vision of earning £5,000 a year. £100 a week, I thought, was crazy when the weekly wage at the time was about £7! However, he did eventually make it a few years later. Another RAF kitchen orderly was 'Tich' Francis who as his name suggests was about 5' 2' and from a working-class family. I gave him a life to his home in London on my way to my girlfriend's in Streatham, and was nonplussed to find his family using orange boxes for chairs and tables! I still have a photo of us three at the rear of the officers' mess, looking like the 'I-know-my-place' trio from the Two Ronnies sketch.

Three techniques I learned from the civilian chef and not to be practiced at the Connaught were: (1) cleaning potatoes for baking—tip a 28lb bag of Jersey Whites into a pot sink, ½ fill with lukewarm water, and with a large yard broom, scrub the said potatoes until free of soil. Rinse and place on trays ready for baking—quick and simple. (2) Omelette mix—take two trays of eggs (72) and tip into a Hobart (large mixer) including shells, feathers, and whisk until well mixed. Strain said mix of shells etc. through a conical strainer (we called them comical strangers!) and bingo—omelette mix. (3) ACC (Army Catering Corps) Jelly—take one tin of evaporated milk and chill. Mix two packets of flavoured jelly cubes (raspberry preferably) into two pints and chill. When almost but not quite set, whip the evaporated milk in the aforesaid Hobart mixer on high speed and gradually trickle in the chilled jelly. This will turn out a consistency similar to raspberry mousse and will make about fifty portions as 95 % of the content is air!

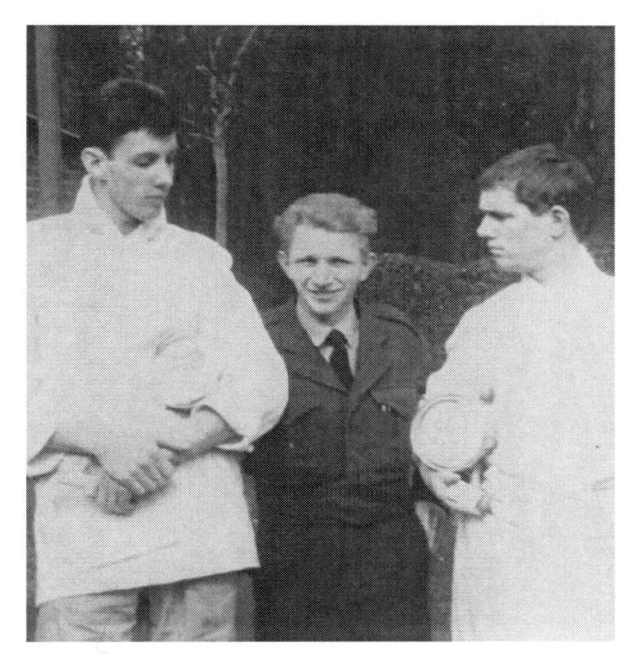

RAF Officers Mess Chefs—L-R Robin A Flynn, 'Tich' Frances, Me *'I know my place!'*

Dale's 22nd birthday welcome by National Service buddies. (me in hat) RAF Bomber Command—1959

Winning the RAF Senior Cup 2—0 with 2 Chelsea players Barry Sluman and Charlie Nicholas. I'm front row 1st left. 1960.

Promotion and Management Training at Acton College

Eventually after, I signed on for an additional twelve months—in reality ten months—to get extra pay and to finish my management exams. I was made up to a Corporal Technician and given charge of a billet. This was not an onerous task, and had the added benefit of having my own room—small but cosy—in the same block. One rainy, cold night on the 26th February (my birthday) returning from my management course at Acton College in London on my newly acquired 350cc BSA motorbike at about 10 p.m., I looked into the billet to see if anyone was around. I had hardly opened the door, when there was a rousing 'Happy Birthday' rendition from the officers mess crew. The billet was decorated with bunting and candles, and snacks and drinks had been laid on, all of which brought a big lump to my throat. It was the most unexpected surprise and celebration I have ever had for a birthday and just summed up the camaraderie that existed between the National Service conscripts. For the same birthday, my twenty-first, my Dad sent me a package of a lovely bottle of wine and a tin of cheese straws. Unfortunately, the bottle arrived in rather small pieces, although the cheese snacks were intact, and fifty-one years later, I still have the tin, which serves as my needle and thread box!

One of the most useful benefits of National Service or service in the Armed Forces was free education. The RAF paid for all my Hotel & Catering Management course fees at Acton Tech. as well as other vocational courses. In addition, I did not have the inconvenience of travelling from the RAF base to examination centres in London an eighty mile round trip as the training officer (T/O) had the authority to invigilate all my exams on the base. In addition he gave me an additional time allowance if it was necessary! 'Just let me know when you've finished' the Pilot Officer would say. One course I was keen to complete was for the Advanced Waiting Certificate as I never had the opportunity of studying restaurant and bar skills at the Connaught. So I contacted Slough Technical College only to be told they required minimum numbers of eight to start, and had only two at the time. A number of other waiters in the officers' mess were interested so with the agreement from the Base's T/O, I called the course tutor at Slough to tell him he had minimum numbers for his waiting course, and naturally he was delighted! So each week, we would cram into two Ford Consuls and drive the thirty odd miles to Slough. During our time there, we also used to help the college with extracurricular functions as barmen. Once, in particular, at a Christmas Party for Aspro Nicholas we were able to generate some badly needed additional earnings, some not entirely legitimate. No one complained, however!

Time Off with My New MotorBike—BSA '350'

Shortly after joining the RAF, I resold the Francis Barnet, and with the help of my girlfriend's father, Ron Valentine bought a second-hand BSA 350cc twin with a go-fast faring for the enormous sum at the time of £60, another bargain. Ron also offered to replace the big end in the engine, and within weeks, I was off to Shaddoxhurst in deepest Kent to take possession of my pride and joy. By the time I arrived in Kent in October, the nights were drawing in, and when I left to return to London, it was dark. The village was in the deep countryside a few miles from the A20, my route of choice, and I was keen to return to Streatham and my girlfriend's bedsit that evening. Shortly after starting out and without warning, I came to a sharp right hand bend and, because my headlights were poorly adjusted, couldn't decelerate fast enough. The bike and I took off, straight over a ditch, through a blackthorn hedge, and crashed into a ploughed field. I had only ridden three miles on my new bike! A local farmer heard the crash and came hotfoot to see what happened. He helped me get the bike back on the road and straightened the handlebars. I adjusted the headlights beam to ensure I did not repeat the excitement and checked nothing else was damaged including myself. The only casualty apart from the bike was a couple of rents in my tough leather airman's jacket which had saved me from more cuts and abrasions. I carried on with no further incidents until I reached London's Streatham Common to Angela, my girlfriend and had a well-deserved hug and beer.

Holiday Jobs with the Army and MotorBike Accidents

On one of my RAF leaves, I worked for an army camp in Norfolk, involving field cookery and had teamed up with an RAF colleague. On our way to Thetford, the BSA developed a leak—the break fluid line had fractured so, no fluid no brakes. We parked at the roadside miles from any town or village, and I sat down to think. My personal philosophy has always been 'there is always an answer to a problem, and if you haven't found the answer, you haven't thought about it long enough'. The fractured copper line had 1 cm diameter, and after awhile, I looked at the bungy straps holding our luggage. The hooks had a protective plastic tubing marginally less than a 1 cm diameter—eureka! So after carefully easing the tubing off and on to the fractured brake line, the two ends were joined. I kicked the bike into life and *bingo*, problem solved! The temporary repair lasted for months.

Three other motorbike incidents occurred during my RAF period and two during my bi-weekly journey to Acton College, one in the winter and one during the summer months. Early one Tuesday evening, as I rode towards Hanger Lane on the A40, I was passing a line of traffic in the dark when suddenly out of a gap in the line of cars on my left appeared a cyclist, or at least his front wheel. To have braked on the wet road would have slid my bike into the cars on the other side of the road so I kept going, crashing through the cyclist's front wheel. I should have stopped, but the inevitable delay would have made me late for college. He should not have crossed at that point so what could I do? I just hoped that he was not injured.

In the second incident, I was riding towards London in June, and shortly before Uxbridge, I felt something lodge itself inside my crash helmet near my right ear. Fearful that it could be a wasp or bee, I instantly let go of the handlebar and crushed my hand against the leather side of the helmet feeling a soft crunch. When I arrived at the college, I removed my helmet to find the remains of a rather large hornet—another close shave!

The third potential disaster occurred near Christmas in 1961. I had left my girlfriend in Streatham on the BSA to travel up to North East for the holidays and had ridden less than a mile when without warning a car shot out of a side road at Streatham Hill Station. The road was icy and downhill so when I braked the bike slide from under me and careered towards the car, which stupidly had braked when he saw me. I ended up wedged under the car's offside with me under the bike, which fortunately was raised above my legs thanks to the bike's crash bars. Apart from being slightly traumatised, I was uninjured, a bruised buttock apart and carried on my 300-mile journey to North Shields with only a dent in my gun-metal cigarette case as a result.

Moving up to Four Wheels

Later in my RAF service, I decided to move onto four wheels so took some driving lessons in High Wycombe. The instructor told me to take my test in uniform as it had a positive effect on the examiner, provided you do not run over anyone during the test. He must have been right as I passed first time in the school's car and rode back to the Mess where the other airmen were waiting to hear the good news. My first car arrived a few months later at a cost of £20, an old black and very large Triumph, which I drove for about six months before selling it on at a small profit. It was just too expensive to run on my £3 weekly RAF wages. Going from the sublime to the ridiculous, I then bought a BMW Isetta 'Bubble' car—a two-seat 750cc four-stroke engine with joined rear wheels and door that opened at the front. A local garage allowed me to remove the engine and replace the piston rings and big end, which had worn rather badly. In those days, cars could be serviced and repaired relatively easily when accompanied by a workshop manual.

Wedding Bells for Corporal Technician Lyons and Angela Valentine

My wedding day at St.Stephen's church. Westminster. London. L to R. Veronica (Angels's sister) Val Valentine (Angela's father). Angela. Me. Dad (peeping out). Bernard (my brother) John Flint (my sister's husband). Bridesmaids were daughters of Angela's friend. September 1960.

Dale (23) & Angela's (21) wedding day cake cutting (made my me of course!) at Mrs. Connelly's in Victoria, London 1960.

Towards the end of my service, my girlfriend Angela and I decided to get married after three years thinking about it. It seemed a good idea at the time, although I recall having cold feet about the decision, but in 1960 one had to do the honourable thing. I had earlier mentioned Mrs Connelly my ex-landlady from Victoria with whom I had kept in touch, and she kindly agreed to host our wedding reception, as we were not exactly well off. All the families came for the wedding in St. Nicholas' Church in nearby Rochester Row, that is Angela's family Val. Ron. Veronica, Keith (who had Down's syndrome) & Brian, Aunty Millie, and my family: Dad, Brother Bernard (best man), Cherry and sons, Simon and Chris, who were our pages. Other friends of Angela and some airmen from the RAF mess. I baked and decorated the cake, of course, and everyone packed in Ma Connelly's front room for the reception. An RAF friend took some photos, although we had some posh ones taken in a studio later. We left Victoria on our honeymoon in our Bubble car for Folkestone where we spent the night overlooking the channel in a rather pleasant hotel and did what newly married couples do, after we had dinner and went to bed! The date! 2 September 1960. The next day, we took the Ferry to spend two weeks in France and Spain—Hubba! Hubba!

The first night in France, due to ferry delays, were spent in the rain, in a tent, in a field somewhere near Calais. Thereafter, the bubble car behaved itself, and we enjoyed lots of chamber d'hotes and small hotels one of which left a very special memory. We arrived in this tiny village in the Loire region and got the last room in this routier hotel named appropriately 'Le Petit Robinson'. We wandered around this beautiful, quiet village until dinner time and returned to a restaurant full of locals and had a tasty meal of beef steak and the best pomme lyonnaise I've ever tasted. Shallow fried par cooked sliced potatoes and onions in clarified butter and garnished with chopped parsley—delicious! I just wish I could remember the village. On the way South on 'D' roads (off motorways), we dropped in at vineyards and chateaux, lunching on bagettes, cheeses, ham, and local wine near rivers and lakes.

Our first visit to Paris was a sobering experience as in one restaurant, we ordered our meal, and when the vegetables were served, we waited ages for the meat until the waiter asked what was wrong? We then discovered that we should have eaten the vegetables first—it was the French custom! For all of the 2,000 odd miles the Isetta behaved itself except for one potentially serious incident. We had briefly visited Barcelona at some friends of Sam, one of our lodgers in the Victoria bedsit. They lived in the mountains near Monserrat, an amazing rocky outcrop near the Pyrenees. Even Napoleon gave up on capturing this vantage point topped by a monastery. The Spanish couple had a house where small iguanas climbed the bedroom walls. They also made soup from mountain herbs and oil, which was quite delicious.

Problems in the French Pyrenees

On leaving, we made our way over the Pyrenees on our way to France, but the car did not like the altitude and struggled up the gradients like a marathon runner at the twenty-two mile mark. Eventually the Isetta made it with not much to spare. We had just ended the mountainous twists and turns near terminal drops with no walls and were descending into the valley close to Toulouse. I looked into the rearview mirror after the car had lurched to one side and what I saw beggared belief. A wheel had detached itself and was following us up the road. It had sheared off the rear axle so we would not be going any further that night!

A young boy had seen what happened, so in my basic French I asked where the nearest garage was. He arrived back with his father who took us and the car to his home. We then learned that the missing pinion would not arrive for two days. In the mean time, he very generously offered to accommodate us as there were no chamber d'hotes or hotels nearby. His job as an engineer was working for the regional electricity board and knew the area well. He was astounded to learn we had just driven over the Pyrenees in a bubble car. Later we dined with them and their two children of six and eight years who also drank the local wine, watered down, of course—quite a surprise. The local garage duly fixed the sheared axle, and we took our leave from our Samaritans and stayed in touch for many years.

Chapter 5

A Start in Catering Management, 1961-1962

Early Management Days in London

After two years' exhaustive study, I took my final HCI (Hotel & Catering Institute) examinations in management and, to my surprise, passed first time. My accounts paper was the weak link, but I figured as long as I balanced both sides all would be well. In addition, the mess stewards and I all passed the waiting examination at Slough College—a double header! My National Service was coming to an end, and by this time, Angela and I had moved into a basement flat in High Wycombe. The accommodation was dark, damp, and in pretty poor condition overall, but fortunately it was not for long. I then turned down an offer to extend my service in the RAF, and we were off down to London and to another of Mrs Connelly's bedsits in Victoria with shared kitchen.

On leaving the RAF and handing in my uniform, I was given my discharge papers and a Certificate of Service saying I had been a Junior Technician—wrong, I had been a Corporal. That I had undertaken instruction duties—wrong. That I had, during my service passed City & Guilds Catering exams—wrong. I passed those before joining up. However, my Commanding Officer Squadron Leader W. G. J. Merrifield wrote 'Cpl. Tech. Lyons is a good and capable cook. He is well able to manage the preparation of rather elaborate meals required for formal luncheons and dinners'—well at least they got that right! My RAF assessment showed me to be a fairly average airman. For example, my air force conduct was *very good* but for the rest, that is, ability as a tradesman; supervisory ability; and personal Qualities, I was only *good*. I wondered what you had to do to be *exemplary*? Anyway, I was now demobbed! Years later, I often wondered why they had not offered me a commission to keep me in service especially as had passed my management exams, which later allowed me exemptions on my Open University degree. It was their loss!

I had applied for many jobs during my last weeks with the RAF and had an offer as a trainee manager with Express Dairies, who had a range of luncheon restaurants and tea shops in and around London. They were similar to Lyons' Teashops serving breakfasts, luncheons, and afternoon teas and closed around 6 p.m. Monday to Saturday, which suited me as a trainee with weekends off. I worked in two operations during my six months, first at their branch near London Bridge in the City and finally in one just off Victoria Street Westminster. I could not see a big future with them as the fare was pretty basic, and my catering skills required more of a challenge.

The next job was with a Wimbledon-based Contract caterer Management Catering Ltd, again as a trainee manager in their staff restaurant at Taylor Woodrow's HQ at Hanger Lane on the A40 near Wembley. After four weeks, I had convinced the area manager to try me out in a small canteen in nearby Acton as a Chef Manager catering for about forty staff with a tea and snack trolley service. The operation was lunches only with three staff and myself doing the menu planning, ordering, cooking, and catering accounts, in fact a one man band at a salary of £10 a week, a very fair rate in 1961. It was a challenging job with prospects as the company had a wide range of industrial units in the London area. Occasionally, suppliers would call to take orders and push their products and would ask for 'the Chef'—I reminded them I was 'the manager' being very self-conscious at the time of my new found status and the fairly low esteem attached to chefs at the time. Now, of course, I am proud to have been a master chef, trained at the Connaught and consider myself on nodding terms with Gordon Ramsey if only at London Marathon and Great North Run starts!

Early Promotion to Brentford

I had been less than six months at Acton when I was asked to take over a larger operation in Brentford on the Great West Road doing 100 + lunches with a staff of twelve. I would now be a proper manager and must have impressed my area supervisor at the time. My new salary was an increase of 20% to £12 a week, a very good wage at that time. There were three dining rooms at Alltools Engineering—one for the factory workers, one for the office staff, and one for the directors and senior managers—status was everything in the 1960s factory dining rooms! In addition, there were three trolleys services for morning and afternoon teas so it was quite a notable increase on the Acton operation. Initially, this gave me many sleepless nights, worrying how I would cope and how I would handle the (imagined) problems of such a large operation. In the event, I developed a no-worry strategy, which I still use today fifty-five years later. In short, stop worrying about things you can't do anything about. I also had my own cashier/bookkeeper called Mavis, who was very adept at getting rid of salesmen unless they had an appointment—a bane of all catering managers. The job was challenging and enjoyable as you had to balance food costs to fine limits while at the same time keeping the customers and clients satisfied with the quality, variety, and attractiveness of the menus and service.

We were into 1962, and London smogs and 'pea soupers' were a regular feature of London life in Autumn and Winter. Traffic would crawl along at about 4 mph as you could not see more than a few feet so getting from Brentford to Victoria involved a bus and tube journey of two hours plus. In the summer mornings, there were regular sightings of swans and geese landing on the A4, which required the RSPCA to remove them. On sunny mornings the reflection off the tarmac gave the swans the appearance of a lake. What a shock it must have been for the birds expecting a nice watery landing and instead getting blistered feet!

First Holidays Abroad in Italy

During this time, we had our first holiday visit to Italy, and as flying in the 1960's was still a bit of a luxury we went by train from Victoria. The destination was Rimini, a seaside resort near Venice. What I remember at the start of the holiday was the fun-people we met on the train. We seem to have laughed all the way to Italy with our fellow passengers, but despite promises to meet we never saw them again. The hotel itself was luxury—all marble and chrome—a million miles from our tatty bedsit in Victoria.

We toured the area visiting Florence with marble everywhere including the main rail station where we had our first pizzas—absolutely delicious!. Venice was also a revelation with the museums full of oriental masterpieces such as samurai warriors' armour and swords encrusted with precious stones. Venice, centuries before, had been the centre of East to West trade building up the merchants' fortunes in the process with spices, silks, gold, silver-ware, and jewellery.

I even obtained a valuable memento from the Doges palace—a wooden doorstop now sadly lost. The most poignant memory was on the Bridge of Sighs where condemned prisoners would be given their last view of Venice through the portalled windows on the bridge—hence the Sighs! On a day trip, we also visited the smallest country in the world with the worst football team! San Marino is tiny but beautiful, dotted with villages lost in a time warp and people that seemed to be born old and creaking. No building seems younger than the fifteenth century, and the churches, despite the summer heat, had a gloomy but cooling restfulness. It was with heavy heart, we returned to our tatty Victorian bedsit and grimy smog-ridden London, resolving to look for a better life—and we found it a few months later!

CHAPTER 6

THE AMERICAN EXPERIENCE—EMIGRATION TO THE USA, 1962-1965

Sailing Away to The New World and A New Life

A brilliant idea for 'a better life' came from Angela. We were very unhappy with our accommodation and dissatisfied with the UK's standard of living. It took months to get a telephone, and to get enough for a deposit on a house was dreamland. So she said, 'why not emigrate to the United States? We've enough for the fare, sufficient until we find jobs and with a far better standard of living in America, we could make enough to afford a house on our return say in two or three years. I was already committed by the time she finished so we set off for the US Embassy in Grosvenor Square and settled on New York City as our first destination. The US authorities were quickly assured we were not communists, had transferable high-level employment skills, a good standard of education, and had enough money not to be an embarrassment to the US Government. They also liked the English and had a flexible quota so visas were quickly sorted. But then Angela got cold feet, and doubts crept in. 'It's a big step and I won't see my family and friends for years, and Americans are not very friendly etc. etc.,' she complained. I quickly thought of the solution. 'I'll go first, sort out some accommodation, get a job, and then call for you to follow—what do you think?' Not a lot as it transpired. 'You're not going on your own. I might not see you again, and in any case, I want to vet any long-term accommodation.' I thought my 'solution' might work, and it did. Within days, we had bought the tickets on the QE 1 (Queen Elizabeth) liner, bought secondhand trunks, sold all the stuff we could not take, given a month's notice of leaving our respective jobs, and told all our family, friends, of our great adventure. Some were filled with grief (family), some were sorry (jobs), some were sceptical (colleagues), and many were frankly envious but pleased for us (friends/club members). Within a short time, we were embarking at Southampton onto the largest ocean liner of its generation and saying our farewells. Dad could not make it but sent a telegram, which I still have in an album. My best friend at the time Bill Paye was there but surprisingly on our return to the UK about three years later, he never wanted any more contact—aren't some people strange? We were on our way!

The £60 one-way transatlantic cost on the 30 October 1962 was remarkable for a number of reasons. The food was utterly fabulous, and the accommodation equally splendid and comfortable; the facilities and service on board were just amazingly top class even though we were in the budget class. However, the most memorable feature of our voyage was that we might not have arrived in New York but for JFK's (John Fiztgerald Kennedy's) political skills. About half-way across the Atlantic, the captain interrupted our dinner one evening with some riveting and alarming news. The USSR, as it was in those days, was locked in a stand-off with the United States regarding Krushkev's aim to base nuclear missiles in Cuba. JFK was not too happy with having ICBM's located some eighty miles from the United States and decided to blockade Cuba to prevent the missiles being unloaded. In getting 'Brinkman of the Year award', Kennedy made many friends amongst the previously anti-democrat brigade in the process. Collectively, the passengers and crew breathed a large sigh of relief as we finally sailed past Ellis Island, the earlier base for immigrants, and the Statue of Liberty to dock at Pier 42 in mid-town Manhattan. I still have a photo of us dining in the liner's restaurant with an elderly English couple on the evening the blockade news broke.

Immigrants Angela & Dale dining on the Q.E.1 mid Atlantic
shortly before JFK's Cuban missile crisis—1962

New York City Welcomes The British Immigrants

 Leaving our trunks in storage, we took the subway shuttle to Grand Central Station on forty-second Street, and coming up to street level, the real effect of our cultural change kicked in with a vengeance. I look up, and up, and up, and up to eventually reach the skyscrapers summit! The shock of seeing a circle of buildings over eighty stories high was mind-blowing coming from London where the tallest building at the time was St. Paul's Cathedral! The pungent street smells and ear-splitting noise of mid-town Manhattan is unique made up as it is of sidewalk hotdog, doughnut, pretzel and coffee stands, restaurants of every persuasion, steam from the subway vents flavoured with the underground cafes and food outlets, taxis and trucks, and limos blaring 'keep-moving' honks. It was the ultimate noisy, smelly, colourful world you either loved or loathed. And I loved it!

A taxi found us some temporary accommodation in a budget hotel just off 5th Avenue from where we refreshed and found an amazing restaurant. The Belmore Cafeteria had free chilled seltzer water on tap. The food on display was mouth-wateringly inexpensive, and so varied that it took ages for us to make up our minds. I returned to New York after many years and dined out royally again at the little changed Belmore Cafeteria—'if it ain't broke, don't fix it' seemed to be their motto.

Accommodation Luxury in Flushing Long Island

After a short time in Manhattan, we found a permanent place to live in Flushing at the end of the subway line in the Borough of Queens a forty-minute ride from Times Square. After our Victorian bedsit, our new accommodation, 2040 Bowne Avenue was a palace, and took us some time to realise that we could really afford a 'luxury' apartment block only ten minutes from the subway. We signed a lease for a year and were given a free month rent, plus a repaint job on the apartment in our chosen colour of pale blue! The rent was U$80 monthly, and as my first job paid $80 weekly it was only 20% of my wage. Angela's salary as a secretary at NBC (National Broadcasting Corporation) was an extra income of U$70, that we saved. We moved in and immediately made friends with neighbours in the next apartment—a Brazilian and Norwegian couple, who loaned me their car so I could pass my US driving test We had only known them for two weeks! That's American hospitality for you! The next day a Bell Telephone engineer called to ask where we wanted the telephone—I was in heaven!

Cheffing for the First Time in Manhattan

My first job as a chef was obtained throught my HCI (Hotel & Catering Institute) contacts in New York. I was unaware that there were many HCI members all over the world. They put me in touch with a chefs agency who fixed me up with a job in the nightclub of the newest Manhattan hotel, the Americana on fifty-second Street and Broadway. The hotel had only been opened a week, so things were still settling down. The hours from 5 p.m.-2 a.m. in the hotel's nightclub was not the most sociable environment, but beggars can't be choosers, and it was U$80 weekly. Basically I was a veg cook, preparing very simple fare and requiring all the culinary skills of a KP (kitchen porter). In an environment that resembled a sauna, I was sandwiched between a hotplate and a bank of stoves for eight hours. Within thirty minutes, I was soaked in sweat and stayed that way for the entire shift! That first night the jazz legend Ella Fitzgerald was singing in the night club.

Leaving work at about 2.30 a.m., I walked down Broadway to the Times Square subway for the journey home to Flushing. On one occasion I stopped at the Metropole Cafe where in the window was the drummer and jazz icon Gene Krupa an ex-Benny Goodman stalwart looking pretty good playing in his dotage. On another, Maynard Ferguson the ex-Stan Kenton trumpeter had his big band squeezed behind the bar blasting out a beautiful noise. Can you imagine my incredulity seeing in the flesh jazzers I had loved and heard but never in a million years expected to meet? For the price of a $1 beer, you could enjoy first class jazz until dawn!

I lasted a whole week at the Americana, and after my introductory week to US employment I returned to the agency and was offered a job as a pastry chef at the Grand Central Hotel starting at 5 a.m. So instead of arriving home at about 4 a.m., I was leaving home at 4 a.m. This job lasted a few weeks and primarily involved making American cheesecakes in a pastry department staffed almost entirely by Peurto Ricans. This was the only time in a kitchen I knew what it was like to be an ethnic minority! However, I did realise that baked American cheesecakes are the best by a long way, and I've never forgotten the recipe!

Buying Tenor Saxophones in the Bowery

I had always hankered to play the tenor saxophone, so shortly after arriving in NYC, I visited a music shop in the Bowery Downtown and picked up an old Buscher for U$99. I didn't realise at the time that the second-hand horn was over forty years old. Nevertheless it had a beautiful tone and was in excellent condition. Before long, I was taking lessons and making progress. By this time, we had made firm friends with the Buchholtz family and their three children. Christian played drums in a modern jazz group and knew a number of top jazzers in 1963 such as Chet Baker whom he befriended when on hard times. Lee Konitz and Zoot Sims were also associates and top West Coast saxophonists. Chris introduced me to another jazz icon Lenny Tristano, a blind pianist from whom he had lessons, and he suggested I have lessons from Zoot Sims and even enrol part time at the prestigious Julliard School of music. But unfortunately this was not to be as we left New York later that year.

Out of The Kitchen and into Management—Downtown NYC

My second job as a trainee manager was at Pace College just off the Brooklyn Bridge in Manhattan with a firm of contract caterers—Industrial Caterers Inc. Their catering was based on a commissary system whereby food was ordered a day or two before from a central production unit and delivered to each outlet on the day requested. This required zero catering skills because all the manager had to do was to order the correct number of dishes and ensure budgets were met and waste minimised. My manager at Pace was a bit eccentric because on the day the Beatles invaded New York City in 1963, appearing at Shea Stadium and on Ed Sullivan's show we all had to wear Beatle wigs! Mind you, this wasn't too unusual as most of New York was wearing them as well.

After serving two months at Pace my training continued at a works canteen in the Bronx. The workers were so rude 'gimme this gimme that' and no 'thank you or please.' I nearly exploded with anger and frustration being used to English manners. Two weeks later I was allocated to cater at a boys' school in upper Manhattan as temporary manager but didn't get on with the entrenched female staff. I did not see much future in that company either and eventually joined a Jewish caterers owned by two brothers—Jay Sealine Inc. as a trainee manager. My brief acclimatisation was at the Federal Building Cafeteria in Idlewild Airport now JFK Airport in New York City. The pop song of the day was 'It's my party and I'll cry if I want to' so whenever I hear it 1964 returns with the smells and sounds of the Federal Cafeteria.

After showing some promise and ability there, I was soon given my own cafeteria in downtown Brooklyn at the Otis elevator staff cafeteria. There I planned menues, ordered provisions, cooked, served, budgeted, and banked the takings. I had one or two part-time assistants but it was in reality a one man band and an enjoyable development for me in chef management with very appreciative customers. What I recall of my subway journey from Flushing and short walk to the Otis H.Q. was the NYPD Police patrolling in pairs bristling with riot gear. The Chicago Watts riots had spread to NYC, and social upheaval with racial overtones was the norm for quite a while. My family and especially my Dad and Sister were particularly anxious about me after reading the alarmist reports of muggings and shootings in NYC. in the UK media. The fact is that in all the time I spent there working until 2 a.m. or travelling at 5 a.m. or starting work at 3 a.m. in the City's 'notorious' subway system I only once witnessed a street fight at first hand. It is a fact that NYC is a 24/7 city but in my experience a pretty safe one.

As evidence of this, I often took the express subway 'A' Train to Harlem to visit jazz clubs and never once had any problems although much of Harlem was thought of as a no-go area for whites. The 'A' train was made famous by the Duke Ellington jazz classic 'Take the "A" train' (up to Harlem).

Publicity photo as Restaurant & Banqueting Manager age 27 for the Downtowner Motor Inn, State College, P.A. USA. 1974.

Downtowner Motor Inn. State College. PA. USA. I was the Restaurant & Banqueting Manager at the opening in 1964. Under the hotel awning is my Rambler American.

Another Promotion at New York Worlds Fair 1964

Two months after my transfer to Otis, I was transferred to the NY Worlds Fair 1964 site where the company had the contract for feeding construction workers. I was designated the site's operations manager with responsibility for supplying fourteen mobile units with drinks and food. I was less a manager than a gofo, but it was a job requiring organisation, fitness, adaptability, quick thinking, and a work ethic to get up at 2 a.m. Fortunately, the site was at Flushing Meadows adjacent to Shea Stadium home of the NY Mets baseball team and only two stops on the subway. Apart from the units being stocked with hot rolls including meatball heros, filled bagels, Danish pastries (my favourite), and coffee crunch pastries, it supplied really good fresh coffee, despite being made in a 180 gallon urn at the operations centre. The coffee filter for this urn was 3 ft wide and took a 7 lb tin of coffee after which it was transferred into 5 gallon insulated churns to be transported to the various units. It was now January 1964, and the outside temperatures were hovering around 18 f, that is,—14c below freezing so occasionally the glass holding dispensers would shatter when being filled with hot coffee. When unit staff called in sick I would have to take over their units. On one occasion, I was serving coffee to a construction worker with a meatball hero i.e. meatballs in gravy on a French stick, and I noticed he had a startling resemblance to James Cagney, the famous film star of the 1940s. After the rush was over, I chatted to him of his resemblance to Cagney. He told me Cagney was his cousin on his father's side, and he did see him occasionally. Wow, I was really made up with this information for the rest of the week as Cagney was one of my favourites!

Prior to this job as operations manager, an incident occurred that completely soured my relations with Jay Sealine Inc. which up to that time had been good. When I was working at Otis Elevator, I would stop off at the World Fair site centre and hand over the takings which usually amounted to about U$80. One day after I had duly handed the takings to the local supervisor one of the brothers told me the previous days takings had been stolen and that the supervisor and myself would have to repay half each. Naturally I was furious saying I had handed the money over and it was then not my responsibility. My argument got me nowhere so I was deducted the amount from my wages over a number of weeks, $10 at a time which was then a tidy sum. I vowed retribution! So after my transfer to the Worlds' Fair site I routinely recalculated small amouts from the receipts from units and these were never noticed. Eventually I had recouped my $40. and then handed in my notice—job done!

Becoming A 'Good Humor' Man—Ices On Long Island

So what now? I'm unemployed in NYC with bills to pay. Looking for a summer job, I chanced upon an advert for ice cream salesmen with the Good Humor Corporation. At the time, Good Humor ice cream was sold nationwide but only through its street vans. The job involved driving a route on Long Island and selling pre-packaged ice cream from a refrigerated van. Before you were given a route however you waited in line at the depot until a vacancy occurred. You then accompanied a salesman on his route to become acclimatised with the system—without pay. If you proved capable and had a clean driving licence you waited in line again until a unit became vacant. After a three-day wageless wait, the supervisor called me over and told me that pay was calculated at 25% of whatever you sold at selling price. For example, if I sold out and my stock less damaged goods was valued at $100 my earnings for the day would be $25. But, no sales = no pay. I was then loaded up with ices for which I had to sign, given a street route around Floral Park, and at 10 a.m. the depot gates were opened and I was on my way along with fifty other salesmen. Unfortunately, the gates were not reopened until 10 p.m. whether you sold out or not!

In addition, I was obliged to join the Teamsters Union whose president was the feared Jimmy Hoffa who was reputed to have links with the Mafia who Bobby Kennedy tried unsuccessfully to indict on corruption charges. In the event, it did not matter because Hoffa soon after disappeared and never reappeared, dead or alive. Jack Nicholson eventually played him in film *Hoffa*.

With my 'go for it' attitude I proved so successful at selling Good Humor ice-cream that the supervisor gave me a bigger van serving from an inside counter which meant I was covered when it rained. Each supervisor earned a percentage of my earnings so naturally good salesmen were promoted and given larger stocks to sell. I would often sell out on good days before time so would drop in to a pizza concession where I would exchange ices for pizzas.

But my very best sales day occurred one sultry evening as I was having a break watching a softball game from the van. I heard band music drifting over from the other side of the park and was told the local high school marching band was at practise on a nearby field and would be finishing shortly. Getting directions, I drove smartly over and arrived as they were about to leave the field having blown brass instruments for two hours or so. Exhausted and extremely thirsty they fell on my truck like vultures and completely cleaned me out. On returning to base, my supervisor was ecstatic, and next day increased my stock significantly!

To remind me when I was a Good Humor ice cream man on Long Island, New York. I was a member of Jimmy Hoffa's Teamster Union and paid 25% of what I earned! July 1963.

A Trip to Newport for the Jazz Festival

During this Good Humor period we met a musician call Christian Bucholtz and his wife Jeanette at a party on Long Island. We were invited to the party by the person from whom I had bought my one and only US car, a six cylinder Rambler American station wagon. The person who sold it to me was a Dave Brubeck fanatic and modern jazz devotee. He bought a new car and invited Angela and me to Newport Connecticut to run the car in, a round trip of over 1,000 miles. Coupled with this drive was the intention to visit the Newport Jazz Festival one of the year's top jazz highlights. It was a dream offer to which we readily agreed. At the Festival held in a rather tiny baseball park were many of the jazz greats of the day: Dizzy Gillespie, Ella, Miles Davis, and my personal favourites Dave Brubeck and his altoist Paul Desmond. Paul sadly died when he was only fifty-three, a tragic loss to the jazz world and a truly unique talent.

A Limited Return to Football or American Soccer

The jazz weekend over I felt a need to resume my football as I had not played since my demob from the RAF. A team was recommended called the New York Blue Star, which I later discovered was a Jewish team hence the Blue Star (of David). They were a jolly lot and had a mixed bag of nationalities. Two Brazilians, a sprinkling of Eastern Europeans, and me the only Englishman. We were a quite good middle of the table semi-professional side and were paid $10 a win, $7.50 a draw, and $5 for a defeat. I had not played many games when a horrendous tackle put paid to my soccer career more or less permanently. I was in my role of inside forward when a fairly innocuous tackle trapped my right leg under the defenders and wrenched my knee in a painful torque. The right cartilage being badly torn laid me up and out of work for two weeks. Fortunately, the club insurance paid my wages and medical fees and I became a couch potato for a while watching Groucho Marx panel game and his catchphrase 'Say the magic word and win a hundred dollars'.

So back as a Good Humor man and with summer ending fast, I applied and had interviews for various management jobs. One with the New York prison service as a prison catering manager. At the interview, I was told that in an emergency, everyone was enlisted to hunt escaped prisoners—even the catering manager. 'Not for me,' I thought. Another management offer was with Denny's Restaurants, a well-respected and developing restaurant chain that looked promising, but I was expected to relocate to an upstate town I had never heard. So again—no thanks!

Goodbye Long Island—Hello State College Pennsylvania PA

Eventually, I put an advert in the NY Times and had a reply from a consultant who was acting for the Downtowner Motor Inn franchise—a national motel chain. He interviewed me in Trenton, New Jersey, and recommended me to his clients, a consortium in State College Pennsylvania and hometown of Pennsylvania State University.

The consortium wanted to interview me in State College, so they flew Angela and me from Newark Airport in New Jersey in a tiny plane to a very small airport near State College where we were met by the board of directors. 'The Americans don't do things by half,' I thought and was mightily impressed with their style. I could not imagine the same interview happening in England. The following day after a tour of State College, I was interviewed for the job as Restaurant & Banqueting Manager at the still unfinished Motor Inn with full responsibility for all the food and beverage operations. I was offered the job on the spot, but Angela and I decided that we were not too keen being out in 'middle America' 300 miles from New York. After a long debate, it was decided for me to ask for an unrealistically large salary of $7,500 p.a. rather than just say we didn't like the town or location. Unfortunately, they immediately accepted my counter offer so I was not only stunned but stymied!

Management at the Downtowner Motor Inn

So, after two years in NYC, we were on a 300 mile journey with all our worldly possessions squeezed into a U-Haul trailer and into the unknown. The Motor Inn manager Bob Dennehy helped to sort out a comfortable apartment for us on arrival, and as the Motor Inn was being fitted out, there was plenty of preparation to do in conjunction with the consultant. Menus, equipment, furniture,utensils, crockery, cutlery, and stock ordered. Staffing for the kitchen and restaurant was advertised locally except for the chef who the consultant appointed—big mistake! For three weeks it was all systems go in preparing for the big opening.

State College had a population 20,000 and a student body of about 18,000. The annual college football games attracted crowds of 70,000, and the whole town's traffic system had to be changed to cope with the visitor influx. This happened five times annually, and naturally, all the hotels were at 100% + capacity. Another consideration for my restaurant was that the whole district was 'dry' except for beer, wine and spirits were off limits. Our 'wine' list comprised twenty brands of beer including Guinness and Bass and a 'blind eye' was taken to hard liquor in paper bags in the restaurant, especially during college football weekends.

After the opening one of my biggest thrill at the Motor Inn was to meet the great Max Roach and his band who were staying at the Inn. They were having breakfast one morning when I was on duty, with the group playing at the University the night before. Roach had been the driving force behind many of the great Dizzy & Bird albums, so he was in the top echelon of the modern jazz greats of all time. He seemed very impressed that an Englishman had such admiration for him and his music, and after a brief but enjoyable chat Max and his group signed the menus. What a memento for me!

The Downtowner job was beset with problems from the start. There was regular interference from the wife of the managing director of the consortium into the restaurant operations. Also the consultant had the ear of the board and insisted on keeping the original menus which were too pricey and unexciting. He also hired a chef who was neither skilled enough nor motivated enough to work at creating attractive dishes. I did however create some attractive English specials, hot and cold buffets and gave some talks on catering to hospitality students at the University. One students asked me on viewing a cold buffet 'but how do you get that beautiful red colour on the lobster?' 'Just drop it in boiling water' I replied tongue in cheek!

Life in Middle America

Angela had taken on a job as a secretary, and I became a member of the PHRA (Pennsylvania Hotel & Restaurant Association.) who had very high ideals and a corporate philosophy embodied in ten 'commandments' for their members. My big day came when the first College football team played host to the Navy and filled the 70,000 seat stadium. The spectators must have travelled far and wide as the town's population including students was less than 40,000. We had about 130% occupancy that weekend with four to a double room and a restaurant filled to capacity for the whole weekend.

Angela and I regularly visited other restaurants of the association members, and one in particular I remember was the Boalsburg Steak House whose menus I still have. They had the most enormous T-bone steaks weighing over 16 ozs. Mind you, the locals did have big appetites. Back in the Motor Inn, I was becoming increasingly disenchanted with the amount of interference especially as our customers were eating elsewhere, and I was unable to develop the restaurant on more commercial lines. I then heard second-hand that Angela was pregnant, the very day she had learned from the pregnancy test. Apparently, the doctor who did the tests had chatted to his friends who also knew the Inn owners. Small town America did not endear itself to me on this and on many other occasions. The parochialism of the town was very alienating as we were shut off from the majority of world's news and events in that most media (newspapers, radio, and T.V.) was local. This tended to reinforce the locals insularity and narrow focus. Our holidays did help to provide a welcome diversion, however.

Holidays in America's North East

In almost three years in the USA we had few holidays choosing instead to work and save, but those I do remember were indeed memorable. We toured the Pennsylvania Dutch area which was notable for the Amish and Mennonite settlements and their basic way of life. Although rich in finance and land, they rejected electricity and modern society's trappings such as radio, TV, refrigerators, washing machines, or automobiles. Despite these denials, they seemed happy and prosperous despite being dressed in styles reminiscent of the eighteenth century puritans and travelling in horse-drawn covered buggies. We also had a short holiday visiting Civil War battlefields at Gettysburg in and around Washington and were amazed at the shanty town dwellings of the black community areas. Other day trips included Coney Island on Brooklyn's beach with Nathans famous hot dogs and Jones Beach out on Long Island. On a weekend visit to the Catskill Mountains in upstate New York camping we had a near encounter with a family of skunks and a group of raccoons with youngsters in tow who just loved raiding all the camp rubbish bins.

We also visited many jazz clubs & venues, including the Village Vanguard where Miles Davis failed to show but Blossom Dearie stepped in for the evening To Carnegie Hall for the Modern Jazz Quartet and catching Bud Powell on forty-second Street when he was well past his best, but still great. And finally Zoot Simms and Al Cohn at the Half Note where the entrance of $4 included a meatball hero—what a bargain! Another visit concerned the native American Indian runner of Olympic fame Jim Thorpe, who had a town named after him. On touring his museum we were amazed at the bigotry of the American Athletics Association in the 1920's when, they stripped him of his gold medals for a minor infringement of the amateur code. Apparently, he was given a small gift after playing baseball, and this was viewed as 'payment' and therefore illegal and it was only many decades and petitions later that the medals were reinstated, sadly many years after his death. Eventually, a lasting tribute and popular film was made on his life starring Burt Lancaster which went some way to healing the Thorpe family's feelings of injustice. But now it was about time to consider returning home to England.

Cheerio Pennsylvania and the Downtowner Motor Inn

Secretly, I had applied for management jobs elsewhere and had some interest shown by Holiday Inns. So, when the board said they were not satisfied with the restaurant and banqueting business, I offered to resign provided that I was given two months in lieu of notice. This they readily accepted. As we had no medical insurance and medical costs for maternity cover were excessive even if there were no problems, we decided to cut our losses and return to the UK.

It was then May 1965, and shortly before our decision to return, Winston Churchill died in his ninety-fourth year, the greatest Britain of the 20th century. So we packed the trunks again loaded up the U Haul and returned to NYC to prepare for our return trip, this time on the USS America. For the few days before sailing, we stayed with Christian and Janette (Bucholtz) on Long Island's Floral Park. After returning the little U Haul trailer we wrote to our families who were overjoyed by the double good news of our return and Angela's pregnancy!

Compared to our outward journey the return to England was uneventful but, unlike the Q. E., most of the waiters on board were Peurto Rican. As we sailed out of NY harbour and past the Statue of Liberty, I noticed the last span of the new Verserrano Narrows Bridge being hoisted into place, the new bridge linking Staten Island to Brooklyn. This bridge would eventually became the iconic image of the New York City marathon and which I would run over seven times many years later. My lasting impression on landing at Southampton was how small the cars were and that I was deeply unhappy returning to England. Whilst in the United States, I used to have nightmares that I was still in England never having emigrated such was my enjoyment of the American way of life—the 'can-do' society. We both agreed that had we stayed another year, we would probably have settled permanently in America.

Dale & Angela returning to the UK
on board the SS France—1965

CHAPTER 7

SENIOR CATERING MANAGEMENT UK, 1965-1970

Back in the Blighty with a New Outlook

Shortly after returning to England in May 1965, we rented a flat near London's Blackheath to await the birth of our first daughter and to start some serious house hunting and job seeking. Within a couple of weeks I had landed a catering managers job with the caterers Management Catering Ltd. Wimbledon. Reuters and Press Association in Fleet Street was the hub of international news reporting and because of that the staff cafeteria operated with an evening shift until 11 p.m. and on Saturday until 2 p.m. As the catering manager, my wage had risen from £12 to £25 a week in my three years in the States, and with an alternate Saturday, the total of £37 was a very good salary at the time. We catered for about eighty lunches with morning and afternoon trolleys and snacks and had a staff of six on days and four on nights. The night shift was managed by a very attractive lady, who would not have been out of place as a model. On the day shift, I had a chef and an assistant manageress who I hired, and they both proved to be reliable and skilled.

 I introduced many ideas and dishes from my US experience such as pizzas, which had not hit London at the time, meat loaf, cheese cakes, and specialist buffets. After customer requests I even tried jellied eels and tripe & onions without any success whatsoever. This was 1966 the year of our World cup football win and after chatting up some of the Press Association photographers was given a selection of the winning England team and also some of the Beatles in their iconic Sergeant Pepper uniforms. I eventually sold these on e-bay many years later. It was a really enjoyable job and an easy journey from Blackheath to Blackfriars on Southern Region. By this time, we had found our first house in Sidcup at 4 Exeter Road, a 30's three bedroom terrace with a small garden and rear access garage about a mile from Sidcup town centre costing an enormous sum of £4,000 and a mortgage of £2,000. But, we were on the ladder!

Proud New Parents with a Baby Girl

Shortly after arriving in Sidcup, our first child was born on 25 September 1965, Kyla Ondine Lyons 7lb 3ozs in the front bedroom with Daddy helping the visiting midwife and the first to see her! What a result! The house then took priority with decorating and upgrading as the previous occupants had let things slide. I decided to install central heating and contacted the DIY Central Heating Company to provide a quote and discuss the process and likely problems of installation. They provided everything to install a comprehensive system tailor-made to the house, including plans, instructions, and a gas boiler. They even bent the lounge and bedroom radiators to fit the bow windows. Looking back I must have been mad to install a comprehensive gas fired system without any real technical know-how, but I finished it. Altogether it took about three months to install and took up most of my weekends as Angela had Kyla to look after, and I had a full-time job at Reuters. There were a few problems naturally such as putting pipe bends on the wrong way and having rooms off limits while I levered floor boards up and sawed joists to install the copper piping. Surprisingly, when the big day came I switched on and, after a short heart stopping seconds and lots of peculiar noises, the system burst into life first time. Twenty years later and long after I had moved out, it was still operational—amazing!

My job at Reuters was really enjoyable until I had a disagreement with the client over some trivial problem, and instead of just apologising for the oversight, I dug my heels in and paid the penalty. After two productive years, I was transferred out by my area supervisor as they did not want to lose a good manager, and ended up as a holiday relief in another staff restaurant. This move was in reality good experience but not the career move I had envisaged. In the mean time, Angela once again became pregnant with perhaps a boy this time! On 30 May 1967, another lovely little girl arrived with black hair who was again delivered at 4 Exeter Road weighing in at 6 lbs 7ozs. Again I was the first to see Iona Clare Lyons enter the world, in fact for the first few seconds catching sight of the umbilical cord I thought it *was* a boy.

At the time, our marriage was going through its worst phase with serious arguments, usually over the smallest things, but for the sake of the kids, we stuck together. Our daughters were not very happy with the situation either—see Kyla's reminiscences in Appendix 1.—and really our relationship was a separation in waiting, especially as our sex life had also been put on the back burner for some time. During this period I did have some short term affairs but our marriage stuttered on.

Donkey riding Iona looking worried, age 3 with Angela and Kyla (Dinkum Diddler) age 5 at Weston-super-Mare 1970
'the tide and the sun was out!'

My youngest daughter Iona (Tichy-Too-Toughy) age 5
with her favourite bunny at 4 Beverley Avenue
(our first home costing £4,000) 1971.

A Management Promotion in Fleet Street

My search for job improvement went on as the relief manager's job was primarily a holding operation and pretty devoid of any development. After a few more job applications and interviews, I found myself being interviewed for the biggest job I had ever experienced and felt at the time I had bitten off a little more than I could handle. But my modus operandi at the time was 'the only way is up'!. The reason I was eventually offered the job was due to my technical catering qualifications and experience, coupled with my studies for the Diploma in Management (DMS) at the Regent Street Poly. My management experience in the United States was also a contributing factor as well.

I was in charge of one of the largest newspaper group's catering organisation, Associated Newspapers Ltd. off Fleet Street. At the time they owned a string of publications; *the London Evening News, the Daily Mail, the Daily Sketch, the Weekend Magazine,* and the *Manchester Guardian.* The catering department had a staff of 120 in 4 separate staff restaurants excluding the Guardian in Manchester and a director's dining room which played host to such luminaries such as Billy Butlin and Princess Margaret. Lords Rothermere and Harmsworth, the owners, regularly ate there. The newspaper industry was a closed (union) shop i.e. all workers had to belong to a trade union and that included my catering staff who were represented by the T&GWU (Transport and General Workers Union). This actually made my job easier because my staff had excellent conditions of employment and pay for catering staff and security of tenure.

My first day on the job was noteworthy for a special visit I had from the print unions FOC (father of the chapel) who was basically a union convenor with powerful links to the print management. He told me in no uncertain terms that he had given the previous manager a heart attack and that as long as I toed the line with him I would be OK: otherwise, watch out! I thanked him for his advice and asked him what he expected of the catering services which rather took him aback. Subsequently we got on quite well because if I required any favours or extra equipment for the four works canteens, he only had to put in a word to management, and it would be sanctioned PDQ (pretty damn quick)!

Solving Catering Problems at the Sketch and Mail

The initial problems with the catering department were legion. Financial budgets were not in place; food costs were spiralling; staff recruitment and retention were difficult as there were no black or coloured personnel on the staff; menu planning was non-existent, and quality control was slipshod. Similarly, purchasing and stock cost control had no central direction or policy. My first evaluation of the managers showed that they and their staff were competent, cooperative, and keen to effect improvements and were keen to cooperate in the required changes. The exception being the Directors Dining Room Chef whom I later replaced. My only office staff, a secretary cum cost controller was a godsend in that she had been there for years and knew the background to the catering operations, the staff, and the important union chiefs. Buyers for the main suppliers had been given no directives regarding their quality or service, and there was clear evidence of graft. One supplier for greengroceries for example offered me bribes to ensure he retained the concession. Others such as grocers and butchers were giving kickbacks to the previous manager and, for all I knew, to the unit managers as well. The effect of all this was lower quality and higher costs in all our cafeterias.

Finally, I had a review of our suppliers and, with the involvement and cooperation of unit managers, created a new list with at least three choices for each of the main suppliers—grocers, fishmongers, butchers, greengrocers, and non-food suppliers. Competition for our business, which amounted to £'000's weekly, would create cost savings and improve quality as a consequence. Menu planning using fresh seasonal foods was encouraged, and monthly menu planning was submitted to my assistant manager for checking and approval. Each week we had a unit meeting and a general awareness review of developments and problems/ issues. A Catering Committee was formed involving T&GWU., print Union shop stewards and other interested parties, and we met on a monthly basis to air concerns and provide feedback on catering in their areas.

Within months, costs plummeted as budgets were agreed and action taken on improvements with the agreement of unit managers and this resulted in improved food service quality to customers and fewer complaints. On staff recruitment, I instituted an open-staff selection policy, and within weeks, we had a healthy application list of black ladies. A print union rep. heard about this change on the grapevine and said his members would not like their food being handled by black catering staff. I told him that we did not have the luxury of being able to pick and choose staff, and in any event, catering operations country wide ran effectively because of and not despite of black workers. If they wanted better service, they would have to accept the new policy, but they were free to eat elsewhere if they were that concerned. In the event, our black workers became customer favourites, and if print union members gave them a hard time, they were immediately sanctioned by their own staff to behave or else! My 'friendly' print Shop Steward FOC was particularly helpful in this respect as he had no truck with members who he labelled 'racists'.

Improving Rapport with the Print Unions

As price increases were a definite no-no by the unions, one particularly satisfying example of cost cutting without any customer complaints was the significant savings on eggs. Each case of eggs contained 360, and I noticed the invoices were always for large eggs, so I asked Mary my unit manageress at the Daily Sketch, a no-nonsense Irish lady, whether we could try standard instead of large eggs. She was all for this, so we ordered a test case, and surprise, surprise, there were no complaints or uproar from the union FOC's. The resulting savings were significant as the weekly orders were for ten to fifteen cases weekly, that is, about 4,000 eggs! Mary's customer rapport was summed up in her disarming response to late grumblings at the lack of choice. 'You have four choices my dear' she would smile as customer expectations rose; 'there is that or nothing, take it or leave it!'

The next major union opposition was to drink and snack vending. This area was one of my targets for moving the catering forward in all canteens and operational areas as many of the print department were a long way from the canteens in the Victorian buildings. The only vending was cigarettes, and there had been many examples of damaged units and thefts from machines. As a result, I moved these from isolated corridors to the canteens and more populated areas. Although the unions Shop Stewards were anti-vending for entirely subjective reasons, I convinced them it would not result in staff reductions, in fact quite the opposite. In addition, I argued it would provide more employment and provide extended services when the canteens were closed, by the provision of drinks and snacks. For this development I hired a retired J.Lyons sales manager for to oversee all the vending, that is drinks, snacks, cigarettes and tobacco. Being older and wise enough to handle the young and streetwise print employees Fred did a great job, especially as he was the boss and really pleased to get the job. In addition, the extra sales generated helped to balance budgets and improve cost control. Eventually, we increased the number of vending machines to thirty within twelve months, with the agreement of the print unions.

In my role of General Catering Manager for the Associated Newspaper group, I was asked to check out the Manchester Guardian catering facilities and rode north on the Manchester Pullman one weekend. My report was not overly critical on quality and costs, so they were given the green light to continue without any of my continued involvement. I was not unduly concerned as I had enough on my plate in Fleet Street.

A Vending Solution at Commercial Wharf

One year into the new job I was given the responsibility of overseeing another operation on the South Bank at Commercial Wharf where some copies of the Weekend magazine were produced. It had a tiny canteen run by a small semi-skilled staff, mainly providing snacks and drinks, but it was out of date, a health risk, and inefficiently run. The unions wanted a major revamp of the facility and this also fitted neatly into my game plan for development. In addition, many complaints were made of the food, service, and unhygienic premises. My reputation for improved quality on the North bank had filtered to the Commercial Wharf workers and they were pestering management for a change. At the time, I was studying for the DMS and had to complete a major project linked to my employment. 'What an opportunity to develop a revolutionary catering operation based entirely on vending principles,' I thought. This had the attractive ingredients of lower staff costs and tighter cost control, so the management were all in favour. As a result, I was given a budget of £3,000 for the redevelopment, and of course, the unions were very supportive as they were getting a brand-new canteen with the promise of improved food and service and even better, management were having to spend large sums on their behalf!

I involved Zanussi, an Italian catering equipment company to help me design and install an upmarket range of vending machines and catering equipment and also to monitor my method studied designs to ensure the production flows were accurate. In addition, to ensure that product quality and service was up to the main canteens standard I appointed the assistant manager of the Daily Sketch canteen who was adept at handling the unions. She was delighted with the promotion and readily accepted. The end result was a win/win for all concerned and helped me pass my DMS project with flying colours.

A Diploma in Management and the European Cup for Man. United

After presenting my final project, I had the satisfaction of seeing Best, Charlton, and Law take Benfica apart in the European Cup final 4-1 after extra time. Best scored a hat-trick, and I passed the DMS—what a year! At work, I had been given a new boss who was an ex-union official and had been promoted beyond his competence level—a clear case of the Peter Principle in action! At the time, I used to have a day off in the week to play golf with Angela's sister's husband Tony as sometimes I had to work weekends or come in on the occasional evening. My new manager was not happy with this arrangement and expected me to be at his beck and call whenever it suited him. At about the same time my request for a pay rise to David English, the general manager was received with a high level of petulance, saying he decided the timing and amount of salary increases and not his managers. Naturally, I was fuming as I had reduced food costs substantially, saving them tens of thousands of pounds and had improved the all-round quality and efficiency of the catering services. That was the last straw, so I decided then to look elsewhere for more appreciative employers and satisfaction. And before long an unexpected opportunity appeared on the horizon.

CHAPTER 8

MOVING INTO FURTHER & HIGHER EDUCATION, 1970-1977

A Career Opening with Part-Time Lecturing

A colleague I met at a catering manager's conference suggested I try some part-time teaching at a local college as he had used this method as an avenue into full-time lecturing. So 'nothing ventured,' I thought, so phoned a few London colleges including my old alma mater Westminster College. Eventually, after a few calls I was given some part-time lecturing hours at the Borough Polytechnic in South East London—now South Bank University. I was told the catering management students had a few weeks left of their course but had finished the formal syllabus so, could I give them eight sessions on my experiences of the industry in order to help prepare them for the real world. In the event the students really enjoyed hearing about my work both in the UK and the United States especially when I worked in New York City and the pay was excellent—£15 per hour in 1969 was very welcome. So, whilst still at Associated Newspapers, I applied for a full-time lecturing position at Hendon College of Technology, soon to be Middlesex Polytechnic.

'They named a village after me!' Dale at Dale, Wales—1976

A New Career in Teaching Opens Up

Surprisingly I was short listed for the L.2 / Senior Lecturer position and at the interview, was competing with only one other, a lecturer from another college who naturally was very confident. He had not reckoned with someone with management qualifications in trade and general management, the DMS, and who also had senior management experience in the catering industry. The Head of Department, David Wilks, wanted someone with good trade experience coupled with management experience, so I was duly appointed a Lecturer 2 in management studies. I taught all the Higher National Diploma and Hotel & Catering Management students in addition to human resource management with IPM (Institute of Personnel Management) students.

I was surprised and delighted to be appointed at my first attempt and promptly handed in my notice. The management at Associated Newspapers were not amused, but they only had themselves to blame for treating me shamefully over my conditions of employment. The catering staff were also very sad as I had established a really good working relationship with all the managers and staff, and in that respect, was sorry to leave. With just over two years at Associated News, I was now off into Higher Education—another career move beckoned—in the Department of Hotel & Catering Studies in September 1970. Living at 4 Exeter Road Sidcup was a ninety-minute journey to Hendon underground compared to the forty-five minute journey to Fleet Street. But, as I was just about to start on my Open University Social Science degree course, I was able to use the extra journey productively as study time and always found a seat on both rail and tube travelling as I was against the commuter traffic flows.

Although I was designated a general management lecturer with the bulk of my teaching within the Hotel & Catering Department I was nevertheless occasionally drafted in to fill-in to teach Management Studies on the Institute of Personnel Management course in the Business Studies Department. This teaching was very satisfying because these students wanted to learn about management. In addition my examples from the Hotel & Catering Industry were much more easily assimilated, as everyone has experience of hotels and restaurants.

Tea at Auntie Sadie's with Dad, Me, Auntie Sadie and
Bro. Bernard. South Shields. Co. Durham Sporting my
University style of long hair and viva Zapata moustache. 1975.

The Trials of a New Lecturer

And then the curse of teaching struck me. I had only been lecturing for two weeks when I lost my voice! It was a clear case of too much talking and not enough getting students to do things. So I bought a book entitled 'What's the use of lecturers,' which clearly indicated didactic teaching was basically a waste of time. Too little was understood or recalled based on research studies. In short, the book was MBO (Management by Objectives) related to teaching and was a godsend. Gone were the piles of carefully rehearsed notes and in went student study objectives linked to learning outcomes with lots of hands on examples. The students set their own learning objectives and, in many cases, marked their own assessments, which were often marked more critically than mine! After this change of emphasis my voice quickly returned!

Apart from my ten hours weekly lecturing, most of my time was helping to organise industrial placements for students doing sandwich courses. Six months had to be spent in a related industrial outlet such as a hotel, restaurant, or industrial catering unit. We had students in London's top hotels such as Grosvenor House; The Savoy; and The Ritz. But I still cannot understand why I did not even attempt to place them at the Connaught, the base for my own training.

Setting up, monitoring, and liaising with industrial managers, although time consuming was rewarding and satisfying and kept me up to speed on industrial developments. In addition, it also helped to open up avenues for consultancy and research. This was high level job satisfaction!

Research Opportunities in Hotels

In fact, a short time after starting at the now renamed Middlesex Polytechnic, I was asked to do some research with Holidays Inns on labour turnover with Colin Dix a work colleague. We broadened this research to embrace Job Satisfaction and linked it to research by Frederick Herzberg, the behavioural psychologist. We eventually did compare Herzbergs findings with two Holiday Inns, one in Swiss Cottage London and the other in Tyne & Wear near Newcastle. The research was an eye opening to the hotel management and resulted in a number of sweeping changes to the staff environment, conditions of work, and management structures. Two most surprising conclusions were that higher levels of job dissatisfaction were recorded for staff uniforms and staff meals—higher even than for wages. Later a similar piece of research with hotels in the Birmingham area was the basis for my Masters Degree in Social Psychology at Birmingham University, but more about that later.

The teaching environment at the Poly was very relaxed with a teaching pool in the Department of about fifteen lecturers, half of whom were catering practitioners in kitchens, housekeeping, hotel reception, and the public restaurant. The remainder were lawyers, economists, marketers, and myself in general management. Students in the main were industrious, bright, well-behaved, and from a mainly WASP (White Anglo-Saxon Protestant) background.as ethnic minority applications were rarely received. Each year in the Department we had a Christmas party and served luncheon to the students. At this event, the Wooden Spoon was awarded to the lecturer they loved to hate, and one year I was the slightly embarrassed recipient, but nevertheless taken in good spirit. A couple of years later, I took my revenge by creating an award for the biggest PITA (pain in the arse) student entitled the Big Head of Hendon, which in fact was a sculptured male head I had made years earlier in an arts class. Each year, we put a brass plaque on the base with the student's name. After initial complaints from students that it was demeaning, the Big Head eventually became quite a status symbol for the student selected and continued many years after I had moved to Birmingham.

I spent over seven very enjoyable years at Hendon & Middlesex Poly, later to become Middlesex University and really should have stayed. But my yearning for more self-development and 'achievement motivation' to quote Herzberg was irresistible as I entered my late thirties.

Winning the National Catering Business Game

The same reason (achievement motivation) was my initiative to enter a student team in the National Catering Business Game. This involved making financial decisions in regard to production, marketing, personnel, and accounts within a virtual catering organisation. Students from the HCIMA Management Course were entered in 1974 as the Middlesex Poly Dodgers (after the Brooklyn Dodgers) and duly carried off the trophy against thirty other UK catering colleges. Two years later teaching staff were allowed to enter the industrial section of the game so along with three colleages I entered a college team. The Game involved ten weeks of postal competition after which six finalists were selected for a weekend final at Stafford Poly. With me as Team Leader we won on the final decision with some inspired marketing decisions. Our prize was a beautiful silver-plated medallion in the shape of a maze designed by the English Tourist Board, who sponsored the event and a silver rose bowl. The medal sits proudly in a cabinet along with my other sporting trophies.

Shortly after joining Hendon, I also took up squash and became a keen competitor at a club close to home. On one of my industrial visits, I met a young lady working for Gardner Merchants, the largest UK industrial caterers at the time. She was the training manager and placed quite a number of students for me with very good outlets. Eventually, she became the training officer at the Grosvenor House (GH) Hotel in Mayfair and contacted me to arrange student placements in their kitchens. This was an exceptional training establishment because GH was the only hotel in London that had had a trade union.

On one of my visits there, I met their new Personnel Manager, Philip Thompson, a Cambridge University graduate in Philosophy, not the usual educational background for a hotel manager. Philip had started as a management trainee at the Dorchester Hotel just around the corner in Park Lane and some years later after personnel work with housing charities, was appointed at GH. We became good friends, and shortly after our meeting, I organised a team-building weekend for him with senior managers in order to improve team development. This area had been, in the GM's opinion, a major weakness, contributing to falling standards in the hotel. I put a great amount of thought and time into the role-play exercises and case studies relevant to the perceived issues in the hotel. As a result the departmental managers response to the two days was a positive and enjoyable experience.

After the workshop, we were invited to a special dinner at one of Forte's top restaurants in Regent Street and were surprised that after the dinner Ray Carrol, the GM, gave all his managers a roasting and warned them their jobs were on the line! Some end to a team-building exercise!

During this time, I was also heavily involved with my Open University degree, completing unit assignments, attending workshops and Summer Schools, all of which was tough but rewarding.

Middlesex Poly 'Dodgers' Winners National Catering Business Game L-R Stan Speigel & Dale (long hair) & HCIMA Students—1974

CHAPTER 9

THE OPEN UNIVERSITY YEARS, 1970-1990

Stepping up to my B. A. Degree

During my time at Middlesex Polytechnic, I enrolled on the degree programme at the newly created Open University (OU), the brainchild of Jenny Lee a pioneering labour cabinet member in the Wilson government. One year after the OU's start, I was accepted onto the Social Science programme in 1971 with the first foundation unit D100 Understanding Society. I was immediately hooked onto all this new learning and in-depth projects. The tuition included weekend seminars, study sessions with tutors, and summer schools at top universities York, UEA (Norwich), Nottingham, and Sussex (Brighton) which were a revelation. For my second level units, I studied Systems Management which included a week's summer school at either York or UEA. It was pretty intensive study, but after five years hard graft, I was handed my B.A. (Hons) 2.1. Social Science diploma by the principal of Middlesex Poly. This was in the concert hall, adjacent to Westminster Abbey. Definitely a very proud moment in my life and just like the Strawman in the Wizard of Oz I had proof of a brain!

In my O. U. study group at Sidcup had been a young man who was keen and sporty, and we hit it off immediately. Dick (Richard) Delisle was a civil servant with a local authority in Surrey, and we both had a passion for squash. We would play regularly in Orpington and, being competitive types, would compete for supremacy and often end up with colourful bruises. Over the years, he become my main London Marathon supporter and best friend.

In the same group was a young married woman called Valerie, who lived near Bromley. We also hit it off as she was unhappily married, and I was in the same position. Before long, we were very close and seeing each other on a weekly basis. Her husband's job had moved to Bristol, so she had to relocate after a year, so our meetings became less frequent, although I did visit on a number of occasions with Kyla and Iona as she had three children about the same ages.

My Marriage Ends

My full time lecturing at Middlesex Poly was definitely the most enjoyable job I had ever had: with one long round of enjoyable companions, a satisfying love life, and a great job with prospects of promotion.

Unfortunately, it was not matched by my home life, which was deteriorating fast into a final separation. We just could not agree on anything, and our frequent heated arguments occasionally became little more than 'handbags at ten paces', which must have been very disturbing for Kyla and Iona, who were still very young six and eight year olds at the time. Eventually, we agreed to separate in 1975 and surprisingly sorted out the legalities without giving the lawyers a large grub stake. I then bought a three-bedroom semi-detached at 158 Gypsy Road in Welling from an Indian family for £12,000 in 1975, and it took me months to rid the house of rice, cooked and uncooked. They must have eaten in every room, including the bedrooms!

The new house had a very long garden with a lean-to conservatory at the rear and ripe for development. But apart from a good clean up and a modicum of decorating, I did little renovation or modernisation in the three years I lived there. This was partly due to studying for the Open University degree and my full-time job at Middlesex Polytechnic where I was now a Senior Lecturer. In addition, I entertained my daughters every other weekend and sometimes during the week and was still involved with Valerie, the Open University student. What with holidays with Kyla & Iona and my part-time work as an Open University tutor on the D100 Social Science foundation course, there wasn't much time for house DIY.

Angela and I agreed that the kids would stay with her at Beverley Avenue and that I would see them most weekends. Sidcup was only fifteen minutes from Gypsy Road after all. As I recall, Angela was unable to get much of a mortgage on Beverley Avenue, so I took less of the 50 % value of the house, a tidy sum with the understanding the difference would be settled if and when she sold.

Kyla and Iona seemed to accept the inevitable as they would have separate rooms when I left with another house to explore, and no more parental fisticuffs. They would also have a dedicated room in my new house. Iona seemed to make the adjustment quicker than Kyla so with a new mortgage to pay and an agreed monthly amount for the girls upkeep to pay, I needed to generate more income so took in a lodger in the shape of Mike Tucker. He was an accomplished yachtie and worked for Shell as a computer wizard. Since then we have kept in touch and have had many great days and weeks sailing to France and the Channel Islands.

Open University Summer Schools

I was now an established student and tutor with the OU on both systems and social sciences. On one occasion, I was inadvertently allocated to myself as my own counsellor! This anomaly arose because I had a student number and another number as a tutor, in itself rather unusual. The computer programmes at the time were less sophisticated and could not cross-check my dual status. I was getting paid to counsel myself in effect and had been given confidential files on myself by other tutors and counsellors, some not too complimentary. Months later, a letter came to say 'due to an administrative error we will be reallocating you to a new counsellor'. I'll bet there were some red faces at the OU control centre as a result.

I eventually became a tutor on Systems and on the Social Science Foundation Course for the O.U., as well as a counsellor and Summer School tutor for a number of years. During these Summer Schools, liaisons were a regular attraction, and I was no exception. In fact, sporting a Black Tutors Badge was often a magnate to female students.

Summer schools were a bonus for staff and students alike especially young mothers who were free of husbands and household chores and made the most of it—socially in particular. On one occasion a young mother developed a serious liaison with another student and, at the end of the week, refused to go home, sitting on the steps and crying. Eventually, her husband had to be called to take her away! On another occasion, a couple agreed to meet the next year having established a close bonding the previous year, but when they met up again, the women found someone more desirable in her tutorial group. This process of self-discovery and awakening was well documented in the popular film 'Educating Rita' starring Michael Caine and Julie Walters as an OU student. She realised through her studies and her relationship with her tutor (Michael Caine} how empty her life had been and eventually left her husband. It has to be said that O.U. Summer Schools had, in my experience a deserved reputation for easy, short term sexual encounters with mature, frustrated mums a prime example—and beneficiary!

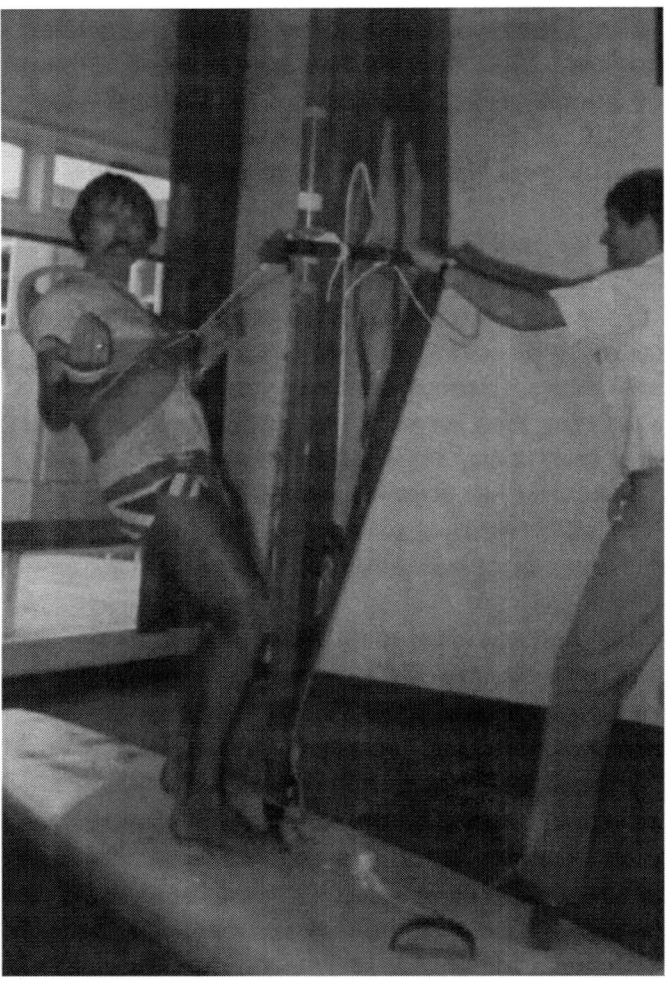

Systems tutor Dale giving a 'dramatic' evening seminar at York University OU Summer School using a windsurfer to demonstrate systems concepts. 1986.

As an OU Summer School tutor, I was allocated twelve students on the Systems Management course for the whole week. The first day was spent bonding with the group, involving many clever ice-breaking exercises. One of which was for each student to give a detailed account of themselves adding what they thought was special about them. Initially most said 'I'm not special,' but given a little nudging by myself and the group, some students were indeed very special—one of which had been the co-pilot on the first Concorde flight!

Many permanent relationships developed from these groups, and some students retained links with me for years. I still get Christmas cards from an ex-student in Jersey, and Janet, my partner, recently talked to an Inner Wheeler Jill Joyce who remembered being in my student group at UEA (Norwich) in the 1980's—I must have been very good or very bad!

Chapter 10

Skiing—A New Sport & Partners, 1975-2010

Exciting Challenges and Potential Disasters on the Slopes

During this time in Welling, I took up skiing with a vengeance and with an assortment of friends and family travelled to resorts in Austria, Italy, France, and Spain (Andorra). Some of the resorts I remember with affection were Macunaga, Sauzi d'Ouze, Bormio, Livignio, Alpe d'huez, Zermatt, Val d'Isere, and became a reasonable Black Run skier. The famous black runs were The Wall in Avoriaz; The Canneloni in Madessimo in Italy, and the Mont Fort in the Haute Savoire. Both Kyla and Iona became accomplished skiers and would occasionally follow me down a black run, protesting that I had told them it was a red (easier) run!

I have had some near catastrophes in the process; the most alarming and near fatal one happened in the French Alps in Chamonix. I had left a College of Food wine study group in France and headed for Geneva in Switzerland and then by train on to Chamonix. On this particular day, I had teamed up with a Frenchman, and we were skiing high up when a thin mist came down, and we were separated. I skied on and lost the piste markers only to realise I was near the edge of a precipice on snow with an icy coating. Unable to get an edge, I slid towards the edge frantically digging with my poles for purchase but without any success. 'This is the end,' I thought—as I plummeted over the edge into oblivion.

My fall was arrested about forty feet down in deep snow and only yards from gigantic boulders. Dazed by the fall, I tentatively felt my legs and body for any serious injuries, but all seemed in order. My skis however had gone. One was thirty feet away below me and broken in half while the other jutted out of snow forty feet above my head on the precipice edge. What an escape! 'Someone up there must like me,' but how do I get back with no skis—I'm off piste and at 8,000 ft with no reference point. Eventually after fifteen minutes or so, I spied some off piste skiers a long way below and called 'au secours! au secours!' and waving my only ski stick hoping they spoke French. They eventually acknowledged my distress and skied away to get help. Hoping I didn't die of hypothermia before being rescued I thought, 'how lucky I'd been and that I could have become just another ski fatality statistic and labelled a silly risk-taker'.

However, the 'blood wagon' basically a metal sled duly arrived in the hands of two mountain rescuers and, after strapping me in, careered down the mountain much faster than I'd ever skied. The waiting crowds at the cable car station were terribly disappointed when the straps were undone I athletically leaped out—ta dah! Later I received a bill from the ski authorities for 8,000 fr., which I am ashamed to admit I am still intending to pay—thirty years late! My broken ski came home to Wadleys Road and stayed for many years on the outhouse wall. Another hairy ski run and definitely *not* for the faint hearted.

Sking the moguls in Tigne, France, Haute Savoire—1983

Skiing on The Glacier in the Valle Blanche Chamonix

Earlier that week, I had heard of the longest run of 15 km in the Alps—the Valle Blanche. Unfortunately, access to the run was via the highest cable car in Europe, the Aguille du Midi. You were strongly advised to take a guide and to have crampons, ropes, and ice pick as there had been many fatalities on the approaches to the Valle. I did take crampons but no guide, reasoning I thought, to follow a group *with* a guide—no problem! I emerged from the cable car and through a tunnel in the rock to be faced with the scariest nightmare of anyone suffering from vertigo.

The ski area was down a metre-wide ice stairway of fifty metres with a single rope for balance with terminal falls to oblivion on either side! Taking a deep breath, I looked straight ahead and gingerly negotiated myself to the first platform. A kind instructor volunteered to take my skis down, but once at the ski-off area, my skis had vanished! Panic wasn't the word as there was no way back and no way forward without skis. 'They have to be here,' I reasoned, looking around, and, after what seemed ages, I glanced up the ice steps to see my skis on the first platform! Eventually after shouting myself hoarse, another guide heard my cries and delivered the skis and a 'merci beaucoup Monsieur' from me and much to my relief.

The next stage was to negotiate the Salle a Manger which is a series of crevasses around which you have to ski with extreme care. In the past, many animals and skiers have disappeared into these crevasses never to reappear! Another ten minute skiing, and I was onto the Valle Blanche proper by which time my chosen 'group' had disappeared. You are literally skiing on a glacier and can see, underneath the snow the beautiful emerald blue ice. The skiing is an easy blue standard, with a very wide piste so you can admire the phenomenal scenery of ice cliffs towering on either side. The eeriest thing however is the total absence of sound except your own breathing—complete silence. No birds, no animals, no skiers within range, no traffic, nothing! Totally unique and in a way alien because, in normal living we are never, ever without surrounding noise of some kind.

Later on, I saw a film about extreme skiers, and one group had skied from the top from the ice stairway *straight down*! The pictures were shot from an adjacent mountain, so one could see these specks skiing down what was almost a vertical face—definitely not for the vertiginously challenged! Prior to my adventure on the Valle Blanche, I had heard the story of a skier who had apparently committed suicide by skiing straight off the top, never to be seen again! I did go back once more up the Aiguille and had a long walk at the end because I went later in the year, and the snow had regressed up the glacier by about a kilometre.

Trading up to the Black Runs in France and Italy

With my friends Philip and Mina (Thompson), Pat, Rosie, and Sue, we went to Madessimo in the Italian Dolomites and I nearly perished on the Cannaloni a black ski run. On the way up, my guide succumbed to frostbite and had to return in the gondola, leaving me to make my own way back. It was late in the day, and the strong wind had removed the ski tracks on the piste. I thought 'don't panic Mr Mannering' and, at one stage had to remove my skis to climb back up to find the official piste but by that time the slope police had long gone. I eventually returned to the resort hours later, arriving back just before dark after all the lifts had closed. Sue and my friends were close to panicking and gave me a good telling off! Quite right, one should never ski black runs without support.

The next year both Kyla and Iona came skiing with us: first to Avoriaz in the French Alps and then to the Swiss resort at Mayerhofen both great fun and not without some nerve racking black runs. One of the toughest is The Wall a fearsome black run in Avoriaz between France and Switzerland that has claimed many lives. The first thirty metres are almost vertical, but with plenty of snow you can traverse your way down but it is a long way and very tiring. On this occasion I unofficially joined a 30 plus group and eventually made it back to the resort, despite some *very* hairy moments and threats by the leader of the group to abandon me.

On another occasion, Kyla got very cross with me when the lift back to our Swiss resort closed due to high winds, and we had to ski back down a black run from Avoriaz—she made it with some style after I told her it was an easy 'red' run. Morzine was the sister resort in the valley, and one day Iona and I did the 10 k Elephant trail a normally green/blue (easy) ski touring route. Unfortunately, the weather closed in with snow and whiteouts until we could hardly see the signposts. Iona was only fourteen at the time, so it was a credit to her skiing and resolve that we made it back to Morzine before dark!

I still don't know how we got four into that apartment in Avoriaz (Iona, Sue, Fiona (my lodger in Wadleys Road) and yours truly), quite a squeeze. It was so tight we had to get dressed two at a time and the 'kitchen' allowed only one person at a time, so not surprisingly we ate out most of the time. Eventually that holiday ended with the cable car from Morzine closed due to high winds, and we had to clamber back up the mountain an elevation of some 1,000 feet carrying our skis—quite a hike! The wind in this purpose built resort was so fierce that you had the feeling the apartment blocks would be blown away! However, fabulous snow conditions existed for the whole of our ten day Neilson holiday. The return journey to the UK was an exhausting 19 hours coach trip, but it was a cheap option after all.

Me in skiing in Bormio Italy with reflections of Dick. 1984.

Skiing Accidents in Austria

Austrian resorts were very popular in the 1970s, and one year, we went to Mayerhofen with Pat (Churcher), Kyla, and Iona in the spring. It was so hot and sunny that the girls, who were only eight and ten at the time had to wear face coverings and still ended up with enormous blisters. Because the resort was quite low you were skiing on slush in the afternoons, so we stayed higher up the mountain where there were ice bars and good snow most of the day. Patrick was a kamikaze skier with more enthusiasm than skill. On one occasion, totally out of control, he mowed down a group of beginners like ten-pin skittles and just walked away, leaving a line of destruction behind. I was watching this from a safe distance. Mind you, I can't talk because four days into our week, I did something equally silly and paid for it.

There was a very steep narrow path which some experts had gouged out and being a go-for-it skier thought, why not have a go? Halfway down with nowhere to go, I realised the bottom ended rather abruptly uphill with no turn off. I hurtled down into the slope bottom and promptly wiped out big time with skis, spraying in all directions. When I came to I realised my ankle had taken the brunt of the fall because I couldn't stand on it so I slide the rest of the way to the chair-life on my derriere, ably assisted by my daughters. Patrick was off destroying some other unsuspecting group at the time. For the next two days, I spent the time hobbling around on crutches, which I have photos to prove!

Next day the snow was so poor, we caught the mountain railway to Zell am Ziller, and for the first time saw the first RIRO (roll-in roll-out) ski waxing station. For ten Austrian shillings you glided into this covered plastic dome where rollers waxed your skis as you moved through and off out the other side you zipped with goo-fast skis—magic! Another first in the same resort was a DIY slalom course. Again for ten 'A' Shillings you went through a barrier and down the marked slalom course for about 1 km, which timed your run on a screen at the finish. The slowest bought the drinks at the apres-ski bar, and it wasn't me!

Group fun on the slopes and an amazing 'sight'

Another year, I teamed up with a group of like-minded skiers in France near the Matterhorn, and the four of us had a ball. Our competitions were as follows: 1. longest time on one ski downhill, 2. skiing downhill on a red run as a foursome train (usually out of control), 3. skiing through the legs of one or two or three others, 4. longest time skiing backwards and 5. furthest lying down on the skis (murder on the knees however!). We usually ended up in a heap!

On another day, we encountered a woman sitting in the snow wearing a white tabard and a red line through a large eye on the front. We were told she was a blind skier! How does that work we wondered? It was not long before we found out. Later that morning, we were skiing an easy red run and came across the same woman skiing ahead of a man, who turned out to be her husband. Eventually they stopped and we engaged them with a barrage of questions. It transpired they had been skiing together for many years, graduating to red and easy black runs. He would call out instructions for turns, stops, and warnings for easy or difficult terrain which his wife responded to with a high degree of skill. Hey, we thought, let's try it with our eyes shut but found it impossible to keep them closed for more than two seconds! We concluded that you have to be really blind to gain that level of confidence and skill—there's no other way.

The least satisfactory skiing was in Canada near to Banff and Lake Louise. I went with Jeff (Way) and friends in January 2002 for ten nights' room only, so the overall cost was pretty expensive. Each day, we had to coach forty-five minutes to Lake Louise, arriving at around 10.30 a.m. with the lifts open until 4 p.m. The runs were relatively short nor with much variation in slope difficulty. The temperature at that time of year hovered around the—12 c mark, so you had to be well wrapped up and moving.

Our accommodation was two beds for three males, so sleeping arrangements were not conducive to a good nights sleep. To cap it all, the flight to Calgary took over nine hours, so I crossed Canada off my ski holiday list!

My Best and Worst Resorts

Best? Not in any particular order: Tigne, Val D'Isere, and Alpe D'Huez, (France); Zermatt (Switzerland); Livignio, Bormio, Madessimo, and Passo Tonale (Italy);

Worst? Not counting Canada, Scotland (anywhere), Spanish Pyrenees; and Most Austrian resorts (too low) unless you go in deep winter or very high.

Here follows a short report of one of my recent ski holidays in my favourite resort Alpe D'Huez and gives an indication why I find skiing so enjoyable—read on!

High in the French Alps and Not One Snowflake

One week in 2007, I skied and snowboarded in Alpe d'Huez, a ski centre 1,850 meters (6,000 ft) high in the French Haute Savoir mountains near Grenoble. The sky was blue; the snow was deep and crisp, and even but the temperature was a bit chilly at—5 degrees C, but no problem, I had my furlined undies ready.

Fortunately, there were few queues at the drag lifts, ski gondolas, bubbles or 'yogurt pots' (sort of hinged half cages). The green, blue, red, and black ski slopes were wide and long and most had good snow cover—mainly from the big Christmas snowfall. In the resort, there were many free facilities for lift pass holders such as a frequent ski bus, two swimming pools (one inside and one outside), a gymnasium, a night-time floodlit slope, and an ice rink; my dodgy knee precluded the last two—malheureusement!

The hotel, Les Cimes (The Peaks), was well up to scratch and near to the ski runs, lifts, and skibus stop. What a result! The staff were all British, young, entertaining, friendly, and helpful and served up excellent breakfasts and dinners with litre jugs of swigable vin de pays. The bedrooms were enticingly warm and with a bath, shower, loo, and duveted beds, all was cosy. The room's south-facing balcony also had a fabulous view of the snow-covered Alps. What another result!

Around the ski areas, there were skiers, snow boarders, (of course) serious walkers, husky sledges, mountaineers, ski de fonders (cross country), and also skiers on adapted wheel chairs—and going at some lick!

And another result! Yes, we found the Yeti or the abominable snowman on a distant slope. He was frighteningly friendly and a fair old skier too—and no poles!

The best bit though was that booking late online gave us a £600 holiday for £280! The worst bit was a four hour delay at Grenoble on the return due to one extra and unaccounted for piece of luggage. We all had to leave the plane and identify our luggage on the tarmac—in the rain. Oh yes and £6.50 for a fairly average vin chaud.

Despite that, it was a marvellous week with lots of beautiful weather, no sprains, bruises, or broken bones, thank God!

Enjoy, enjoy! Dale 20 January 2009

Snowboarding beginnings—A Painful Experience!

In 1997 at the tender age of sixty, I took up snowboarding—bad decision! I bought a slalom board—only goes one way—with hard boots. I should have got an all-round board (goes both ways) with soft boots. Still I persevered, and with an hour's lesson in the great Italian resort of Passo Tonale, I took off but not before I'd taken some hard falls with whiplash injuries. I then found out the hard way that drag lifts are *not* designed for any kind of snowboards. Also you do not have sticks to pole along when you hit a long flat section. Also falling in deepish snow is a nightmare to get out of so *never* take your board off in deep snow—you'll never get it back on! And always, always, always board with someone else, preferably a skier. They can extricate you more easily from off piste and can also tow you along on the flat sections. Of course, if you know the resort you can avoid most flat sections by using red or black runs. Blues and greens are fraught with long flat sections and are to be avoided. Also, have plenty of padding, especially at the beginner & intermediate stages, that is, around bum, knees, wrist strengtheners, and a helmet. Coming off a board other than from a chair lift, you either fall forward (broken wrists) or backwards (neck whiplash or bum bruises), so the right equipment is a definite pain-reducing value-for-money option.

I am certain that my present stiff neck and arthritic vertebrae are the result of snowboarding injuries over the early years. Eventually, until my right knee became unusable with severe arthritis, I became a competent snowboarder and would attempt most black runs but not without a degree of trepidation I admit. However, you do perfect parallels on a board (ski joke), and a there is a real sense of exhilaration swooping and looping down a long red run, carving turns and spinning the board 180 degrees left or right. I might have been better advised to stick to improving my skiing!

Drags Lists and Snowboards Do Not Mix!

My worst nightmare on the board was in the Three Valleys at the end of a day when I had snowboarded to a sister resort and was on my way back to Meribel. Unfortunately, I was too late to catch a chair so had to take a rather long drag lift. About halfway up I was getting tired and caught an edge of snow. Despite valiant efforts to retain my balance I came off because keeping straight on a drag you are facing across and not up the slope so your legs can cramp up. Also, when falling off a drag, you cannot catch the next pommel because once you've come off the pommel shoots out of reach. I was in the snow, nowhere near the piste and on a steep snowy slope with the top nowhere in sight. I slung the board across my back and dug into the snow with my first step. About thirty minutes later, I reached the top totally exhausted and dripping with sweat despite the icy temperature.

Eventually, I reached Meribel and chalet accommodation, vowing never ever to use a drag lift again unless there was no other way! In 2006, I eventually sold my snowboard but retained my soft boots, still intent on keeping my hand-in during my weeks skiing and so far I have!

Sailing Away Across the Channel

Dale a Windsurfing 'expert' (51) beach starting on the short board at Haverigg Cumbria in the Southern Lakes. We (Sue) had a 300 year old cobble cottage nearby overlooking Morcambe Bay 1988.

Sandwiched between skiing, six of us (Dick, Colin, Mike Doyle, Myself, and a friend of Mike) skippered by Mike, rented a magnificent sailing boat for a week, a Nicholson thirty-two. Sailing from Lymington in Hampshire, we crossed the channel, narrowly missing assorted steamers, freighters, and cruise liners in the process and eventually docked in Le Havre on day two. The weather worsened, so we stayed until boredom tempted us out in a force six. Not a good idea with a raw crew so after almost losing the front jib, we turned back into Le Havre well chastened, with Skipper Mike not amused. On day four, we escaped and motored down to Alderney where we woke to find we were moored next to a submarine, which had snuck up on us in the night. We then spent a very pleasant day on the tiny island and then decided the remainder of the Channel Islands would have to wait as the yacht was due back in Lymington.

On the return leg, all of us, skipper apart, were very sea-sick on the night crossing and I succumbed to a nasty stomach bug feeling like death warmed up. The next day of our return was sailed in glorious weather, which I could not enjoy in the least. The others however, were living it up, catching mackerel by the bucketful, which they proceeded to grill under my nose and take the Mickey as I lay dying—rotten sods!

On one occasion, Mike took three of us to France with my best pal Pat, Mike, and a Scotsman, who played the bagpipes in a kilt when not on duty much to the amusement of the French as we sailed up the Seine. And on another occasion sailed with Mike and his long-term girlfriend Beatrix, a German, to the Isle of Wight for the weekend at Brading. This yacht was the one he and a friend had built in a Bexleyheath back garden! Eventually, they had to hire a mobile crane to lift it onto a low loader which then took it to a South coast marina. Over the years, sailing has been fun and exhilarating!

Dining somewhere in a French Channel resort
on a sailing break with Pat (best mate & deck-hand)
& Mike (Capt.& ex.lodger) 1985.

Liaisons at the Open University

Another one of my female O.U. students on the D100 course, Tonya, was very attractive and lived in Sidcup. She was married with two large Alsatian dogs, two daughters and would come to Gypsy Road for tutorials and counselling. It was not long before our mutual attraction lead to more than counselling, but although the intimate relationship didn't last long, we kept in touch even when I moved to Birmingham. Occasionally I would pop-in for a chat, usually on London Marathon visits.

Another young lady whom I met skiing in Austria's Alpbach came to visit with friends at Gypsy Road and with Mike my lodger in tow, we escorted four delectable young ladies to the local Indian (restaurant). We did get some jealous looks not surprisingly. I continued the link with Brenda who was in the army and visited at her family home in Brighton for a very enjoyable weekend with me sleeping on the sofa and getting nightly visits. It must have been a good summer as I remember we cavorted in the sea for most of one day in glorious weather. She eventually decided I wasn't going to pop the question and married an army sergeant but not before she visited me in Wadleys Road to say goodbye.

A pop song at the time was linked to a love affair that I had with Valerie the OU student, Roberta Flack's 'Killing me Softly'. This relationship deteriorated after I met Hazel, and became rather nasty so I had to send her a solicitor's letter, telling her to stop pestering me. This relationship had echoes of the film with Clint Eastwood *Play Misty for Me* and left me feeling I hadn't acted very well.

In Love with a Librarian

About the same time in 1974 at a UEA Summer School in 1975 I met another young lady called Hazel Abbott who surprisingly was a librarian and fellow Geordie with a family home less than a mile from Dad's house in North Shields. She had blue eyes, blond hair with a reddish tint, a delightful complexion and figure, and a charming personality. Hazel was very good company too, beautiful, sexually attractive, intelligent, and fifteen years younger, but the age difference did not seem to matter. I chatted with her at an O.U. systems football match and invited her to my evening lecture on job satisfaction. What a Casanova! At the time, she was living in Pinner in North London less than ten minutes drive from my work at Middlesex Poly. Too good to be true! Eventually, Hazel moved to South London's New Cross, thirty minutes from Welling. We stayed together for about three years but never in the same house primarily because I didn't ask her to—big mistake! We had holidays galore, in Scotland, camping on the Kyles of Butte, short breaks in the Lakes, and skied in many resorts such as Livingno and Kranska Gora. Unfortunately my girls didn't take to Hazel because she was rather distant with them. Perhaps she resented them coming between us as often they would be with me when she visited—again my fault. Also when I returned to London from Birmingham to visit, it was usually to see the girls as well, which was really unfair to her. I really regret not asking her to marry me or telling her I loved her until it was too late!

We gradually drifted apart, and although I did see her again in hospital when she succumbed to a severe skin rash and again on a visit to her new home near Southport, the relationship had died. We did meet again for a weekend in Kendal a few years later but it was more as friends. Our favourite tune was England Dan & John Ford Coley's 1970s hit song 'I really want to see you tonight'. Hearing it occasionally brings back very happy memories of things that might have been.

Chapter 11

The Birmingham Experience, 1978-1988

Head of Department at the College of Food & Domestic Arts

But I race ahead and back at Middlesex Poly. everything was flowing exceptionally well after six years. I was however considering my future again and 'where do I go from here'—always assuming I wanted to change from a job and work environment I really liked. The Head of Department circuit beckoned so I started applying around the country and did have a number of interviews at well-known catering colleges. Plymouth, Exeter, Leicester, and especially Birmingham where I did not expected to get an interview, it being the biggest dedicated catering college in Britain!

I had the mix they were looking for with 2.1 degree, management qualifications (DMS) in both general and trade management (HMI Finals), and excellent industrial experience both at the grassroots and in senior management with Associated Newspapers. As the department was heavily biased towards practical aspects of hospitality such as kitchen, restaurant, bar, and reception work, my trade experience in all these areas both in the UK and the USA made me a very attractive candidate.

My opposition on the day comprised two principal, lecturers, two heads of department and one with a master's degrees, in short some frightening opposition. The post also carried a significant increase in salary from £4k to £6.5k p.a.! How could I pass that up? With the benefit of hindsight perhaps I should have! Because, I traded a life that was satisfying, close to my daughters, friends, girlfriend, and sporting interests (squash/football); work that was a delight in every way and colleagues with whom I had lots in common for a job I knew little about in a City I had never visited.

Much to my surprise I did get an interview and against all the odds I was appointed in competition with some very high-profile opposition. It took a while to sink in that I had been appointed from a relatively modest teaching level as a Senior Lecturer to the largest department (Grade 6) in the U.K

Sunday Times Fun Run, Hyde Park L—R. Pat, Kyla, Dale, Phil, Mina—1985.

Problems in College Management

Here I was going to an alien environment with other heads who were jealous and suspicious of my position and with staff who, in the main, had idolised my predecessor, Louis Kline. They considered me a bit of an upstart, intent on changing a department that they were comfortable and satisfied with. What a challenge! But biting off more than I could chew has always been my *raison d'etre*.

For the first two months, I was accommodated in the sick bay of the female students hostel on the eighth floor of the college while I completed the purchase of a house at 14 Wadleys Road Solihull The detached house cost £24,500—an enormous sum for me in 1978 although I had sold my house in Welling for £15,000 so had little qualms about meeting mortgage paymets. The college girls made me quite welcome, even though they were less than modest at times, traipsing around in their scanties. Good job, I wasn't a sex maniac! The Principal John Newcombe was disabled from a stroke suffered some years earlier and, as a result, was not really up to the job so took great care not to rock the boat. My main protagonist, Ms Murphy, the Head of Domestic Arts regarded herself as a mother hen to her female staff, some of whom were very attractive and would take exception if I liaised with them on matters of artistic development for my department. The remainder of the College was approximately half the size of my department which had sixty full-time lecturers with 50% food and beverage staff, including chefs and waiting staff, and 50 % management, business studies, and languages. My senior staff team of three principal lecturers were Rodney West, Deputy Head, Ken Rudge, an economist, and Mike Bates, an ex-chef. As the department was training students for the hospitality industry, the second floor held all the practical kitchens and chefs staffroom. In order to give students practical industrial experience, there was also a public restaurant and bar on the ground floor catering for about forty customers daily. On the fifth floor, a student refectory channelled the output from the practical kitchens as well as supplying meals for college staff in the eighth floor dining room. The production residue was sold off at cost or less in a shop on the ground floor to staff and the general public. Orders for these kitchens came via a basement stockroom. It was the individual chef's responsibility to keep within a specific budget, although this was not too closely adhered to as I discovered early in my tenure. It was clear there was a lot to take in and a lot to find out before I could consider any plans for the future. The rough ride was about to start!

A Wedding with an Operatic Sopano

My new home at 14 Wadleys Road was too big a detached house for one person, so I decided to get a lodger to help with the mortgage and housework. Graham Hoddinot was the ideal. His work took him away most days, and he loved gardening. Eventually, he left to buy his own house, and when I was invited to his house-warming, I met Susan Ann Kelly a twenty-eight-year-old optical technician, single, and a soprano with the Birmingham Symphony Orchestra choir. After three months wooing her with chilled chardonnay and home-made pizzas, she decided to move from her newly built house in Redditch to Wadleys Road. After a three year blissful relationship and a move to Sunnybank, a new home in Meriden, we agreed get married. So, on 30th May 1984 we had a very low-key wedding at Solihull's Registry Office and a reception at the Manor Hotel in Meriden with her parents, Ray and Dorothy, the only guests. Why didn't I want a 'proper' wedding and why didn't I want my colleagues at the college to know about it? Certainly I could afford one, and although Sue agreed with the low-key approach, I am sure now that she would have enjoyed the glitz and glamour of a more substantial celebration, as it was her first! She was after all very vivacious, beautiful, a seasoned operatic performer, and always smartly turned out. In retrospect, I really should have been more conscious of what would have been best for her, her friends, and family. Bad decision Dale!

After we moved to Meriden and had made good friends with our neighbours, Fred and Mary Wright, they persuaded Sue to sing 'Oh For the Wings of a Dove' at their daughter's wedding in the local church. It was a stand-out performance. On another occasion at Birmingham's Conservatoire, she performed one of my favourites, Delibes 'The Flower Duet' just like a professional!

My Dad was not well enough to attend the wedding, and my daughters had other teenage priorities, though they had obviously been invited. Our honeymoon took us, for a few days, to a beautiful hotel in the Lake District near Keswick, and to my shame on our second night, she agreed to let me watch Liverpool beat Munich 1-0 in the European cup final and Kevin Kegan scored the winner—some husband eh!

With my 2nd wife Sue a gifted soprano. Solihull.
West Midlands. 1985.

Getting to Know My Staff and Delegating Control Systems

My first task at the college was to interview all my eighty odd lecturing and ancillary staff, lecturers in cookery and business studies, technicians, and office staff. I was made aware that Louis had kept finance systems and information very much to himself and, in relation to promotion and special treatments, had perhaps not surprisingly favoured the chef lecturers. I set about delegating much of this decision making to those who seemed competent, willing, and above all interested in improving their position and status in the department. This left me valuable time for development across the department. My office required a priority re-vamp as most of the furniture and décor was stuck in a 1960s time warp. So with the help of the maintenance manager and arts lecturers my office was moved into the 1980's.

Although computerisation was still in its infancy, I unearthed a lecturer at Solihull College who had developed catering stock control software, which could be adapted to our requirements. It would however, have to cope with hundreds of practical sessions monthly. After developing a departmental vacancy, I was able to entice this lecturer from Solihull to Birmingham with the offer of a Lecturer 2 position. He readily accepted, and we were up and running with a comprehensive computerised stock control system in 1980.

The next problem was the main training restaurant's booking system which had seating for sixty at lunchtime with a reservation system that was totally customer unfriendly. For example, reservations could only be booked by phone on the same morning, so only those who had plenty of time, or who were 'favoured' customers could get a booking. These informal bookings were made by the senior restaurant lecturer who reserved places for his 'special' customers. Because of this system, the restaurant often had vacant tables with the result that student training suffered and food was wasted. I installed a simple and quick solution. Reservations could be made any time in advance either by phone, letter, or in person. Customers had to provide a contact phone number and were encouraged to give notice of any cancellation but if they did not they were charged for the meal and placed in a 'naughty customer's book' with the threat of being blackballed. The informal system of 'special customers' was eliminated in the process, and restaurant bookings increased dramatically.

A Master Degree Too Far

Sandwiched between sorting out priorities in my department, I began studying for my master's degree, which had been put on hold after leaving London and my aborted M.Sc at LSE (London School of Economics). As I had been an external student at LSE, I was keen to keep it going despite having moved to Birmingham. Unfortunately, the LSE found out about the move and decided it was impractical. But as I had the LSE support, Birmingham University's Department of Psychology accepted my application, and for four years, I ploughed through a research project on my favourite topics—job satisfaction and labour turnover. With close links to many hotels in the region, I enlisted their cooperation to conduct the research by interviewing their staff. This research was based on Herzberg's motivation theories of job satisfaction and my studies coupled with the hotels labour turnover statistics confirmed his findings on job satisfaction and lead to major benefits for the selected hotels and their staff. After interviews with the Department's Examination Board, which were more like inquisitions, I was awarded an M.Sc in Social Psychology for my thesis. Another major hurdle successfully negotiated!

Graduating with an M.Sc. in Social Psychology.
A long hard part-time slog at Birmingham University. 1984.

The First College Restaurant in Egon Ronay

But what other issues, and problems did I tackle during my six years as the Head of Department? First, I was anxious to publicise the department and college as a centre of excellence, so I contacted and eventually succeeded in getting the restaurant published in the Egon Ronay Good Food Guide, the first college restaurant to do so. Shortly after I arrived I was shown a locked room just off the restaurant called Fort Knox. This held all the largely unused restaurant silverware, most of which had never been unwrapped in the two decades since the college opened. The reason? When the initial equipment lists were drawn up, Louis Klein was told his initial requirements would be halved as the City was economising. He therefore doubled the order, and yes—you're way ahead of me—the entire order was approved. There was no way the items could be returned being stamped BCF (Birmingham College of Food), so into Fort Knox like Rip Van Winkle they slept for over twenty years. Silver cruets, silver toast racks, silver nutcrackers, silver salvers, silver-plated servicing dishes, and numerous other items. My question to the restaurant lecturers was: 'Will they ever be used?' 'Not in our lifetime' was the response. So, what to do? After some discussion with my deputies and the waiting staff, it was decided to auction the items by advertising them locally and to our graduates as mementos the subsequent auction raised many hundreds of pounds which was used to buy equipment we really did need.

My department was also instrumental in being the focus for the development of the Birmingham Good Food Guide. This initiative embraced a wide variety of restaurants serving international cuisine—Chinese, Indian, French, Austrian, and the only English one Jonathons was run by two guys, aptly named Jonathon, which is now sadly defunct. The guide had city wide publicity and an inauguration in the City of Birmingham's splendid executive banqueting suite with the Lord Mayor in attendance. Reporters and photographers from the Birmingham Mail and the trade press the *Catering Times* and *The Caterer* featured the inauguration of the guide, which is still going strong after almost thirty years.

As part of my intention to publicise the Department to a wider audience locally and nationally I convinced Ed Doolan the doyen of BBC's Radio W.M. (West Midlands) to broadcast his lunchtime show from the College. Also, being recognised as the U.K.'s premier Catering College Rocco Forte the hotel magnate presented Graduate prizes at the Department's annual dinner in 1983.

Another *bette noir* of mine was smoking in restaurants, so in 1980 with general support, the public restaurant was declared a 'No Smoking Zone',—the very first in Birmingham and possibley the U.K.

Setting up a Museum of Catering

In 1982, I had an idea of starting a museum of catering, the first in the country. So I contacted the local radios *BRMB* and *BBC* WM, and, resulting from the media interviews asking locals if they had any pre-war kitchen items, BBC Radio 4 gave me a call. As a result, I had numerous items donated. But washtubs and kitchen cabinets (in remarkably good condition) we could not accommodate—we just didn't have the room. I even received a call from the personnel manager of London's Savoy Hotel who were spending millions on a reburbishment and had some Victorian stoves to dispose of, some of which were still in use! I did visit the Savoy and was given a tour but had to gracefully decline their kind offer. Six months later in June 1985, UK's first museum of catering opened in a revamped area next to the restaurant by the Lord Mayor of Birmingham. Initially, there were about 200 items donated, including a Victorian ice-cream and cream maker. I later rescued these because the museum ran out of college space, and sadly, after I left the department, the museum was relocated without any security, and many items were lost or stolen. The new Principal MacIntyre had unfortunately no sense of history!

My department was now moving into the twentieth century with all its goods inwards on computer and all the practical areas with budgets to ensure targets were met.

Reconnecting with American Friends

Having lived in the United States for almost three years and retained links with friends and colleagues, I made contact in 1978 with my friends Christian and Jeanette Bucholtz. Christian had moved to Florida after his divorce and lived in Palm Beach in a beautiful area on the East coast about eighty miles North East of the capital Miami. After a week with him and his new family in roasting temperatures, I visited Cape Kennedy and Disneyworld. The Cape visit included close-ups of the Saturn rockets and a lecture on the importance of funding the NASA space programme to national prestige and the technological spin-offs like Velcro. The abiding memories of Disneyworld were the numbers of clinically obese Americans and the terrifying Space Mountain ride where for thirty-five seconds, I clung on to the thighs of a woman I never met and lost all my loose change! What a place to visit and highly recommended! Disney's sense of order, cleanliness, and the advanced technology of its rides and presentations with robotics and holograms were an eye-opener. I then flew to New York with one of his daughters to see Janette on Long Island's Massapequa Park. I had a very pleasant few days there with her and during that time we became very friendly. We also visited the Twin Towers—the NY Trade Centre, now tragically a distant memory. I returned to the college a little overdue and was reprimanded by Principal Newcombe for my tardiness!

Setting up American College Links

During a visit I made running the New York City Marathon in 1981 I made contact with some New York Colleges with catering departments with the intention of developing future cooperation and links initially with Gerald Griffin the Head of Catering at New York City Tech. in Brooklyn. From these links with Paul Smiths College in upstate New York, Cornel University, and the CIA (Culinary Institute of America), I was able to set up lecturer and students' links and exchanges. The link with City Tech. resulted in the College of Food chefs, demonstrating with some distinction at the 'New York Hospitality & Restaurant Show' at the new Jacob Javits Conference Centre in New York City in 1982 and being awarded a number of Gold medals!

As a result of my visits to many other US colleges in New York, New Jersey, and Massachusetts with catering departments, we developed short-course programmes for US students. These programmes and lecturer exchanges were set up during my time as the College Marketing Director. After my early retirement, degree programmes were developed for our HND students with New Hampshire University and other US centres. I take some pride and pleasure in knowing that my involvement with America in the early days were the sole reason for these and other international links.

During my two years at marketing director, I initiated a visit to the 'Chicago Hospitality & Restaurant Show,' the organisation of which was taken over by the Principal MacIntyre and he excluded me from the visit on the grounds of insufficient funds. Knowing him I should have seen through this deception because in the event, a whole gaggle of department heads, vice principal, chefs, and my ex-departmental heads were included. To this day, the episode still sticks in my craw as without my organisation, the event would never had taken place! I should have stuck my heels in and demanded to be included but I didn't, and to this day I'm not sure why.

ADHOC—The New 'Association of Departmental Heads of Catering'

Another creation which I instigated and which still exists today twenty-four years later was forming an organisation called ADHOC (Association of Department Heads of Catering). As a new HOD (Head of Department) in 1978, I knew little about education management so contacted a number of catering departments around the country to pick their brains. These departments around the Midlands and elsewhere (Blackpool, Ealing, and Bournemouth) had heads who were vastly more experienced. In the process, I decided to call a meeting of Midland heads for an information exchange on the issues and problems that concerned them. The first meeting was in a minivan in the car park of Leicester's Southfields College because the college was closed due to a bomb scare! Five HODs attended the inaugural meeting from Southfields, Stratford-on-Avon, Henley (Coventry) and Redditch.

We agreed an informal structure and to meet on a monthly basis at sister colleges to share information and make our voices heard on matters of mutual concern with the involvement of the Catering Press. Our title, ADHOC, was formed because we met on an informal ad hoc basis, a very appropriate mnemonic as it transpired. Over a number of years, our numbers grew as more catering college heads heard or read about our exploits. We were regularly given column inches to raise issues on such diverse topics as examination bodies such as BTEC, industrial liaison problems, funding cutbacks. When I became a BTEC moderator after leaving the college, I was able to keep in touch with ADHOC developments and was gratified and proud to learn when it went national with the Midlands section becoming MADHOC.

A New Principal Arrives

The arrival of a new principal after two years with the retirement of Principal John Newman spelt a seismic change in the culture of the college. Eddy McIntyre was an ex-chef from Scotland and head of a small catering college. He was smart, devious, and dedicated to developing the college on business grounds and was not too concerned how this was achieved. He rode roughshod over the heads to get what he wanted and gradually replaced most of them mainly by pressurising them with increasing demands on staff and resources. After a honeymoon period, when I got on quite well with him, he decided my department was too big and influential and eventually persuaded me to take up a new position as a marketing officer in Birmingham Education's marketing department.

Helping Train for the Business Tourism Boom

This change was sweetened by the offer of the job of marketing director of the college after the twelve month attachment. The attachment involved developing training courses with other Birmingham colleges in support of the new tourism initiative that Birmingham was developing with aid from the EEC. This was closely linked to the new ICC (International Conference Centre) and the burgeoning NEC (National Exhibition Centre) developments close to the new International rail station and airport.

Birmingham Blossoms with the Conference Developments

Some of these tourism lead training initiatives with sister colleges involved Taxi companies (TOA) with short courses covering simple car maintenance and customer-care training. Most taxi drivers were clueless as to what went on under their bonnets! And breakdowns meant lost business with things they could easily rectify such as low water, oil levels, or punctures. The taxi drivers were also given some basic phrases in foreign languages, so they could welcome French, German, Spanish, and Japanese business visitors and tourists to the City. Another programme of training was providing night-club doormen, i.e. bouncers, with skills in customer care and aggression management. As a result, a number of women were appointed and became very successful. Customer-care training was also given to front of house hotel staff, including waiters and receptionists. Added to my marketing brief was to attract appropriate local and national publicity for these initiatives and having made regular contacts with the local media as a head of department, I was able to develop these links on a city-wide basis.

At the same time in 1988, the city was assembling a bid for the 1992 Olympics, and naturally the marketing department had a major role to play. Many of the merchandising items came into our department which, of course I had as samples. In the event, and despite the fact that our bid was 'technically' the best, it received no support from London or Mrs Thatcher's Government and ultimately failed. None of the political big hitters came in support and the bid went to Barcelona. The merchandising items went on sale at major reductions—T-shirts, badges, pins, pens, mugs, and so on and naturally I was in the right place to benefit.

My New College Post—Director of Marketing

My year was up with the marketing department, so I took up residence again at the College of Food much to the disappointment of City Marketing and to the chagrin of Eddy McIntyre who thought he had seen me off the premises for good! I held him to his promise to become the College's first Director of Marketing and promptly took over the task of coordinating the College courses and sales infrastructure. This meant among other jobs, developing a college prospectus, a college video, and short courses for industry. But how could I do this with little support from the college management (Principal) and even less finance? I didn't even have an office, and there was little interest in getting me one! Pushing a boulder uphill with my nose was easy by comparison.

However, as my Dad would say 'Lyons is the name' and I had been in city marketing long enough to know there were many agencies just dying to hand out funding for educational developmental. It wasn't long before I tapped into enough funding to establish not only a team of marketers, but also space in the college for my team to put down roots. I was able to amass a budget in excess of £100,000 to fund college marketing. Even the principal was impressed! In my two years as marketing director, I engaged a team of three who ran short courses and touted for business around the other sister colleges in Birmingham and with small businesses and hotels. For my part, I reorganised the college brochure with a professional all-colour presentation and hired a hardened BBC specialist to produce a video of the college.

Celebrating a 21st Anniversary

In addition to setting up the infrastructure, the twenty-first anniversary of the college was coming up so I set to and organised a public Open Day supported by all the departments to demonstrate their couses. With support from the press and local radio—after all the college had been opened twenty-one years earlier by the Duke of Edinburgh no less—the publicity attracted many hundreds of visitors on the day. I even organised a college fun run with the help of my running club Centurion Joggers with twenty-one laps of the college. As the previous celebrity was not available i.e. Prince Philip I had to make do with the Lord Mayor of Birmingham!

Next on my 'to-do' list was developing college merchandising, so before long we had college T-shirts, caps, badges, carrier bags, mugs and sweatshirts.

On these was our revamped 'Service before Self' logo 'We try harder!' With my marketing team to develop short courses across the city and within the college, I looked farther afield to develop the college brand. Initially, this took in colleges in the United States with whom I had developed close personal ties earlier. This was partly as a result of our participation in the hotel and catering exposition in New York City. Finally with Paul Smiths College in upstate New York I organised a lecturer exchange—swapping one of our top chefs for one of their business lecturers. After three months in America, he did not want to return!

The College was now an integrated marketing unit with an upmarket glossy prospectus to publicise its products and services to industry, the public and most importantly to prospective students locally, nationally and internationally. I had made my mark!

Early retirement—the best option

My relations with the principal and vice principal, Ray Linforth, were by now permanently soured for reasons they alone were aware of so it was only a matter of time for me to apply for early retirement at the tender age of fifty-two. The deal was too generous to pass up and naturally it was given the full support of the principal, resulting in the education department rubber stamping the deal. I received a lump sum payment of £26,000 and a seven-year enhancement on my nineteen-year tenure in education, ensuring a generous monthly pension of £800 in 1989. And, so long as I did not work in any college in the Birmingham area, I would not forfeit any pension rights. In other words I could take up full time employment elsewhere if I wanted.

My eventual send off from the college was less than spectacular, despite ten years of pretty good service—still you cannot have everything. I did, however, have a private function for close friends and colleagues from the college at the Manor Hotel in Meriden at which I was presented with a beautiful crystal decanter.

So, in summary of my time at the college, I had moved my old department into the twentieth century, organisationally, financially, technologically, and into the computer age. I also took pride in that I had broken down the old isolated departmental structure of the college in coordinating products, services, and marketing with a consolidated brand, locally, nationally, and internationally with regular TV and media coverage in my marketing director role. There was much for me and the college to be satisfied with!

Chapter 12

Consultancy & lecturing, 1988-2002

Solving the Problems of Small Business—Another Career Move

After my early retirement in 1988, I was still a moderator for BTEC visiting college departments countrywide, and while it was no great earner, it kept me in touch with educational developments as well as alerted me to part-time lecturing opportunities. I also had the opportunity to take advantage of the government's educational funding when marketing director, so I was able to tap into these training grants for small businesses. By these channels, I encouraged small catering businesses to train their staff in areas such as customer care, staff motivation, and effective selling at little or no cost to them. On the back of this, I developed my own consultancy, D & S Management Associates with funding from the government. I was even allowed to sign on the dole—for the very, very first time—and take advantage of a training scheme for starting your own business.

During this time, I was paid unemployment benefit of £60 per week, and I was still able to continue my consultancy as well as attend training courses part time! 'Having your cake and eating it' seemed an appropriate analogy for this manna from heaven thanks to the government. With generous sponsorship for office stationary from a local charity, I was able to obtain business cards, headed notepaper, envelopes, a new photocopier, and computer as setting up provisions for my business. Initialled pens with my USP (unique selling proposition) 'Solving Your Problems' were handed out to prospective clients and used for publicising D & S Management Associates.

D & S Management—'Solving your Problems'

My 'corporate' business approach was targeting small businesses, catering companies, and hotels and informing them of the government sponsored training for their staff. This involved applying for matched government loans up to £2,000 and then providing them with technical and supervisory training coupled with management consultancy. I would then bill them for the full amount and accept what they were reimbursed from the government, which meant they paid very little for quality training. In addition, I also completed a number of job satisfaction surveys in areas of high labour turnover where there were problems of recruitment usually in small hotels. Many of these research conclusions were a revelation to employers who had little insight into their staffing concerns. In addition, I organised a number of day seminars in a variety of management topics such as sales techniques, customer care, time management, staff motivation, and assertiveness. One of these was for female office staff from the Post Office, most of whom were totally disinterested in being taught anything and especially by a 'young' man. Financially, it was very rewarding for me but a complete waste of resources for the Post Office.

Around the same time, I became a government inspector for FE colleges at a very generous daily rate of £250. This work lasted for over one year until they dispensed with my services for being too aggressive with college managers—telling them the truth about their failings!

Back on 'the' bike—a Harley Electra Glide

Part-Time Lecturing at Coventry Polytechnic

I then applied to Coventry Polytechnic as a part-time lecturer in management studies in the business school and, due to my background with the Open University as a tutor, I was appointed. Teaching marketing to engineering degree students or to master's degree students from Hong Kong was more an EFL (English for Foreign Students) class and not the easiest of options. The foreign students particularly, really appreciated my efforts to educate them in the history of England, Coventry, and Lady Godiva. I also taught nurses and social workers supervisory studies and departmental managers strategic marketing. In effect, any teaching that was required due to the shortfall in the full-time lecturing staff compliment, resulting from the Polytechnic becoming Coventry University in the Tory, lead University explosion I did. I was lecturing between ten and fifteen hours weekly, almost a full-time load, and when I was offered a full-time post, I turned it down to concentrate on my consultancy. Eventually the cuts in higher education lead to drastic cuts in part-time staff, and I was a casualty. I was still a valuable commodity in further education circles and became an inspector in the newly formed educational 'police force'. I was in clover! A further appointment arose as a part-time lecturer at Warwickshire College of FE in Leamington Spa covering a variety of part-time courses such as NEBSS (national examination board of supervisory studies) whose students were a delight to teach.

Enjoying Married Life Around the World

During this time, Sue and I went to the West Indies for two weeks stopping in Barbados (not very friendly) at a stylish hotel on the coast and drove around the Island's fabulous scenery in a hire car. We even had an underwater trip in a 20 persons submersible. This was coupled with another week in St. Lucia at a luxury beach resort where I do remember wrecking their windsurfer in the surf. It was good fun, drinking milk from green coconuts in the local market and mingling with the locals and cruise ship tourists.

A year later, we flew to the Greek Island of Crete and stayed in a cosy little apartment near the harbour and did all the tourist spots, which included an island that had been a leper colony before the war and later a centre for hippies. Southern Spain, Italian Riviera, Monte Carlo, and Yugoslavia (near a naturist beach where Sue was obliged to become one for a day!) were other destinations during our summer holidays. We were a very good team and enjoyed life to the full. During the winters, we would ski most years with an assortment of friends and family, including Phil, Dick, Patrick, and my girls. The years 1985 to 1995 were really good years, being settled in a delightful village, in a great relationship with good friends, with lots to do and with my consultancy working out well. What could go wrong?

Cheers. Sue (2nd wife) and me in Lanzarote well bronzed. 1988.

My Second Marriage on the Rocks

But then came the bombshell I was totally unprepared for. Before this upheaval, my home life with Sue had been jogging along, but unknown to me she was becoming increasingly dissatisfied with our relationship. And to be fair, I was not acting the part of a loving husband as much as I should have. Sue unfortunately disliked confrontation, preferring to bottle it up. She had recently been promoted to the role of a district manager with Boots Opticians and travelled a wide area of the South Midlands on a regular basis, often staying over when visiting clusters of branches. She then had a rather mysterious illness, which landed her in Solihull Hospital late in 1994, but for some reason had not contacted me until she was actually in hospital with some nervous disorder. It came out later she was having an affair with a married colleague and was torn between telling me and keeping it secret.

Leading up to the split, we had what seemed a jolly Christmas with her family and my Dad in Back Lane and so decided to have a few days break in Chesterfield running up to the New Year, but then her increasing distance forced me to confront her. She then told me she had already made up her mind to leave to be with this married man before Christmas. The song that was popular in the 1980s was Pilot's hit single 'It's Magic' which I heard as I was returning from a jog only to hear Sue's confession which was obviously not magic. Strangely enough, I like to hear this tune and even bought the Pilot' CD! Masochism or what?

So, when Sue left, I was later told by her parents that she was riddled with embarrassment and guilt, mainly because deception and adultery were not in her personal code of morality. She had kept this secret for many months, making herself ill which was the one that hospitalised her. Of course, I never suspected that her illness was because she was reluctant to come clean with me. I really should have seen the signs but *c'est la vie*! Her comment to me when the dust had settled was 'I didn't think you would be too bothered' (about her leaving). Certainly, I could see in the cold light of day that I had a share in the split—in a way taking her continued love, support, and vows for granted!

Saving a Marriage or a Waste of Time?

This revelation hit me much harder than I would have thought mainly because Sue had said she would always honour her marriage vows. I did try very hard to save the marriage, but it was obvious she was set on leaving, and I did not make it easy—becoming very angry and aggressive. Ultimately, I fought against this break-up perhaps too belligerently with the result she left on New Year's Day 1995 never to return—coincidentally, the same day my first grandchild, Joseph (Joe) Peter O'Donnell-Lyons was born!

Her parents with whom I had a close and friendly relationship also had no idea she was leaving. Eventually her father, a lay preacher, collected a few of her belongings but nothing of our shared possessions. Perhaps she didn't want reminding of a life we had shared. Despite another couple of meetings to get her to change her mind, it was the end of a thirteen-year relationship which in all honesty had been very good. My daughters were distraught at the news and my close friends totally bemused by Sue's decision. Her lasting comment was to say our relationship had run its course with the comment 'is this all there is?' Maybe she wanted something new, different, better, more exciting I suppose. I never got her to discuss what she thought was missing or unsatisfactory with our relationship. Maybe if we'd have had children, it would have been different but who knows? Maybe I was clutching at straws? Anyway we eventually divorced on the grounds of her adultery and she paid all the costs. For quite some time after I would have dreams that we were reconciled.

A New Relationship—A Disaster in the Waiting

A short time later, I was involved in another relationship, which I guess was destined to fail from the start, but I was blind to the all too obvious signs. And yes, Angela or Anielcha Evans to give her Polish name was thirteen years younger, vivacious, and quite beautiful who had lost her husband to skin cancer about four years earlier. She lived in Coventry with two teenage sons and worked as a social youth worker with Coventry council. We met through a singles advert with our first date at a pub near Kenilworth Castle and hit it off immediately. Unfortunately, her sons resented me as I could never be a replacement for their father and that made things difficult on my visits to her home. Angela was obsessively jealous and had a very, very short fuse over the smallest of disagreements and would dissolve into tears or rants over what I considered trifles. In addition, she would brook no criticisms and was routinely late for most things involving our social life.

So, why did we stay together for almost five years, buy a house together, even buy another house as an investment opportunity, and go on a number of foreign holidays? Well, I don't really know, apart from the fact that we did have a lot of laughs and good times and did share many common interests. Our sex life was also very satisfying after a shaky start. The 'memorable' events of our five-year relationships can be summed up as follows: a. an enjoyable holiday touring the Andalusian triangle in Spain (Granada/Cordoba/Seville); b. a skiing holiday in Passo Tonale was a nightmare as she had no confidence on skis, was jealous of most of the women in the chalet, and froze on easy red runs blaming me of deliberately taking her on the wrong lifts; c. on a BESO consultancy assignment to China in Chengyang, she gave me little support and continually found fault with even minor issues. It was a big mistake to have invited her on this assignment!

My Dad died on this trip in 1995 at the age of ninety-three so we returned home after only two weeks of the four-week assignment. d. Then after the Trans America run, I met her in San Francisco for a week which was mainly fine, although punctuated with occasional wobblies often in bed! It was another bad decision to have invited her. e. The Great North Run was her inaugural ½ marathon and she did well in finishing despite being completely knackered to finish!

Angela (Anielcha) Evans of Polish extraction, my partner for 5 years who I met shortly after Sue my 2nd wife left in 1995.

Another Relationship Ends

f. We then bought a two-bedroom house to rent in Coventry near the Sky Blues football ground at a cost of £16,000, which for the low price was badly in need of repair. With my friend Bob Cooper, my Back Lane neighbour and DIY wizard, we blitzed the place, replacing the kitchen and bathroom and completely redecorated the house after installing central heating. Angela was a total distraction on the odd occasions she decided to help with the decorating and started heated arguments usually over nothing. The house purchase was another bad decision, but after two difficult rentals, we sold it for £42,000—a very tidy profit. g. We then decided to live together—the very worst of my BAD decisions—and bought Fred & Mary Wright's house next door, Windynook which we renamed

Whitestones. I should have taken Iona's advice! In fact, this move basically ripped us further apart as we couldn't give ourselves space after our regular arguments. After two years, I'd had enough and told her I couldn't live with the continual aggravation. Despite her attempting to save the relationship by getting counselling for her condition, we had gone beyond the point of no return. Eventually she came round and accepted that we had no option but to part so we sold Whitestones—me to Rugby and her to Coventry. For a year of two, we kept up irregular visits and occasional meals, but these gradually petered out. My feelings of great relief on parting were because we never married!

After a period of resettlement in Church Lawford, I started to go to singles meetings and dances in Bedworth & Nuneaton to see what was on offer. But was seriously unimpressed and decided to try the singles columns again, with fairly indifferent results. Then, I met Janet (Tomlinson) quite by accident at the Rugby Rotarians annual ball in 2001, and my life changed again.

Chapter 13

Marathon Mania, 1979-2011

Starting with Centurion Joggers

How did I get involved in marathons? Simple! I decided to get fit to play squash at the Solihull Arden Club and started jogging around the streets near Wadleys Road in Solihull. A two mile jog didn't really appeal, so I found a local club Centurion Joggers in Chelmsley Wood not far away and started to get fit. My first night is worth recounting if only for my surprise. John Walker, the chairman, met me on a Tuesday evening and suggested joining a group who were 'only' doing five miles. 'Bit much,' I thought as this group of geriatrics look as though they would struggle doing five yards. Anyway we set off with me listening and them chatting away at a leisurely 6 mph pace, which for me was *fast*. Of course, they finished still chatting while I was knackered—lesson one learned, never judge runners by their appearance!

Two months later, Dave Emery, a fast marathoner, asked me to do a charity run. 'How far?' was my question. 'Only twelve miles? No way!' I had just started feeling comfortable at five miles. 'You can do as much or as little as you like,' he replied. So, like an idiot, I volunteered, and running twice my longest distance, I duly finished the 12 miles well-bushed.

The 1st Peoples Marathon Chelmsley Wood, Birmingham and my first marathon. It was hot & windy. I hit 'The Wall' at 25 miles but finished in a respectable 3:57. 1980.

Dale with Connie Francis, '60's pop star on Capital Radio before the 7th London Marathon——1987

My First and 'Last' Marathon—Hitting 'The Wall'

A few months later, John Walker organised the first Peoples Marathon around Chelmsley Wood in 1980, and, of course as marathons were cool and the top slot for endurance running and very high on the status scale, I volunteered. Ted Page was another head of catering at Leicester's Southfields College and had run long distances, so we teamed up for training runs in the area. Eventually, getting up to sixteen miles on our longest runs, we thought we were ready for 26.2—big mistake! The day came in September 1980 with a four lap race along the Collector road on the Coleshill bypass with about 2,000 runners. It was blisteringly hot with a fierce wind, and after three laps, Ted had vanished ahead or behind me I wasn't sure. Just in front was a runner with a bag of glucose, which he kept dipping into, while I could only salivate behind dying for a carbo boost! Unfortunately, my latest girlfriend had disappeared with the refreshments. Eventually, reaching 25.5 miles, I hit *The Wall*. For those unfamiliar with this state, you hit what seems an invisible wall in your path. It's as though someone has pulled an energy plug from your body with another step impossible. Basically the body has run out of glycogen reserves, depleting the energy levels to zero. For minutes, I remained rooted until a spectator gave me a glucose drink, and within in seconds, I was off running and finished in a very respectable time for a first marathon—3:56:20! My friend Ted finished well behind me.

Celebrating with my daughters Iona (left) and Kyla after the 4th London Marathon. Festival Hall. South Bank. 1984.

Me and Bobby Moore (deceased) England's World Cup winning Captain 1966. At the ATV studios for London Marathon publicity. A real gentleman. 1985.

No Pain—No Gain!

For about two weeks, I was stiff and ached all over and, due to the sun and wind, my calves were badly sunburnt as well. But satisfaction in the shape of a tiny medal and a certificate were my rewards for what was to be a long and unexpected marathon journey. The first Peoples I decided was to be my first and last marathon. However, in 1981, along came Chris Brasher who decided that London should have its first marathon, so naturally I thought it would be OK to do just the inaugural one. Entry was on a first come basis and fortunately I became one of a select band of about 5,000 who trotted off from Greenwich Park to Westminster Bridge on Sunday 29 April 1981 in bright sunshine. My finish time was a very respectable PB (personal best) of 3:10 just behind a Blue Peter presenter. This was the only marathon when the two winners finished holding hands and were given the same time of 2:11:48 —an American Dick Beardsly and a Dane Inge Simonsen! Sandwiched between the Peoples and London Marathons was one of my toughest—The Masters & Maidens over the Hogs Back in Surrey. I completed that in roasting temperatures in a respectable 3: 38 but was totally exhausted, looking grey and haggard as I had hoped to do it in under three hours. I now had the marathon bug and, in 1981, went quite mad, running four marathons! The second Peoples in 3:18 and the 1st Birmingham in 3:23. During these marathon years, I am not the only one to have benefited by keeping healthy because during this time, I have sponsored a number of charities in races around the world.

Charities Need My Help

The first charity I sponsored was Muscular Dystrophy. This is a terminal wasting decease mainly affecting youngsters. Harry Carpenter the famous sports broadcaster was the team captain for many years, and one year, he was encouraged to eat one of my 26.2 mile pancake for £50 sponsorship and naturally agreed. Little did he realise at the time that the pancake had been held in a secure place as a reserve during the marathon! Most of my sponsored runs have been linked to the London and New York Marathons although the Trans America run for Macmillan Nursers was the exception. Patrons such as Jimmy Saville (Stoke Mandeville), Steve Cram (Barnardos), Princess Anne (Barnardos), Trevor Brooking (Muscular Dystrophy) and charities in memory of sporting icons such as Bobby Moore (Cancer Research UK) have all featured in my 30 years of running. I have tried to support large and small ones, as the sponsorship has rarely exceeded £2,000 at a time so £500 for example going to the Solihull Animal Sanctuary, QAC (blind school) or to 'Bring back the Bustard' charities goes much further than the same amount donated to the major charities. However, the larger ones such as Age Concern, Acorns Hospice for Children or Rotary's 'End Polio Now' campaign and Cancer Research UK have also been sponsored.

Over the years I have raised about £50,000 for over twenty charities with sponsorship from family, business contacts, friends, work colleagues, and voluntary organisation members such as Rotary and Inner Wheel. Running marathons especially the big ones tends to focus people's minds on these causes, and if my bizarre running exploits have helped to bolster the funds, all the better. Apart from tossing pancakes, running three-legged, or with egg and spoon for Guinness Records, I have run with a zimmer frame, on crutches, in wheelchairs, and dressed up as a Bustard (a bird previously extinct in Britain) and, in the process gained some notoriety but more importantly, publicity for those charities. They have often told me that the publicity is often more important than the sponsorship. In fact my double and triple London Marathons were featured in BBC documentaries and, in addition helped to double the sponsorship on those occasions!

With Joanna Lumley star of T.V.'s Avengers at ATV Studios. I was appearing on the Wide Awake show before the 1985 London marathon.

With World champion and Geordie Steve Cram sponsoring Barnardos charity in my triple London (78 mile) run. 1998

Dale Attracts Media Recognition

In John Bryant's excellent book on the London Marathon, entitled *'The History of the Greatest Race on Earth'*, he gives some mileage to the **EVERPRESENTS *(www.Everpresents.org.uk)* athletes** who have run every London. He selected me, in particular, with the following description on page 210.

> *'One of the most accomplished of the charity stuntmen is Dale Lyons, who has romped his way through every London, setting (Guinness) records for pancake tossing, egg and spoon racing, and three-legged running. He has also run the London course more than once on the same day. In 1987, and again ten years later, he finished then ran back to the start. In 1998 he covered the route three times. So Lyons reckons he has clocked up twenty-eight London Marathons in the twenty-four years.'*
>
> *In 2004 this 67-year-old, who calls himself the Galloping Gourmet, ran the London in a chef's hat, tossing a pancake in a large frying pan, in 4:19:55. He said he was slowed down by pancake fatigue and thrown off his stride by being passed by wombles, telephone kiosks, geriatric ladies, Batman and Robin'.*

After meeting John at the London Marathon registration in 2006 he signed my copy of the book with the inscription ***'To Dale, A fantastic man of the London Marathon—Go for it—you're far too young for that zimmer!'*** That year, I ran all the way with a zimmer frame as I was raising funds for Age Concern.

Over the years, my media coverage has now filled three scrapbooks of cuttings from international, national and local media. The pick of which was the double-colour spread of my Bustard costume in the Daily Express on the Saturday before the 2005 London. Another memorable feature was the front page photo in the London Evening News of my double pancake tossing London Marathon in 1989 with the two winners in smaller photos on either side!

Leading the way (very briefly) from the Green Start of the 2002 London Marathon. Just slipped under 4 hours in 3:53.

Running up to the London in 2006, the BBC ran a sixty-minute special which featured me in my Church Lawford kitchen, making the pancake I would toss in the marathon. This coverage often had the effect of generating more sponsorship for my chosen charity, which was the primary aim after all. Although I have to say the attendant publicity did polish my ego a bit!

Triathlons and New York Marathons

Outside of my work commitments in 1990, I was living happily in Sunnybank a five-bedroom Victorian farm house in Back Lane, Meriden, with Sue and two cats Smudger and Sooty, acquired as kittens from the local farm—two for the price of one! They would follow me across the fields on my walks, always protesting when outside their comfort zone, which was about 400 yards! I was also running more and more marathons and triathlons, the Chactonbury cross country marathon for example took me 3.55. Then in the 10th London Marathon, I ran 3.44 for a new World Egg & Spoon record, and a Guinness Book entry for the second time. The first for pancake tossing! My publicity photo sandwiched me with two London marathon winners Steve Jones and Steve Gratton, and I've still got the commemorative sweatshirt! Next was a sponsored Egg & Spoon record attempt around Hall Green for a children's school charity where I failed to beat the record but raised lots of cash. Later in 1990, I ran my fourth New York marathon in 3.57.40, the slow time was due to too much sightseeing the day before, coupled with running the six mile International Breakfast run on the Saturday—I should have known better! Sue and I stayed with Doug and Lyn Stern on Columbus Avenue, close to the marathon finish, and we also visited Jeanette (ex-Buchholtz) and Doug Kramer at their beautiful home among the pines on Long Island.

Ironman marathon finishers in Roth Germany (in sunglasses) & members of the Coventry Triathletes Club. My 2nd Ironman and 1st UK o/50 but missed out on a Hawaii place. 1993

My first N.Y.C Marathon with beard and medal at Doug's
(Stern) Columbus Ave. apartment. 1981.

New York City marathon winners. Paula Radcliffe. Me
(4:44:36:) and Henrik Ramalla. South Africa. At New York's
'Inn on the Park' Central Park. November 2004.

The Hawaii Ironman—A Missed Opportunity

Then in 1991, I ran three more marathons—London in 3.34.50 (no frills), and my first Ironman triathlon at Ironbridge, Shropshire in 12:48. I just missing out on a trip to the Hawiian Ironman by thirty seconds because I tossed a pancake in the marathon—silly boy! Veronica Seyers my friend from Jersey whom I had met at York Summer School, also completed it—quite an athlete! My training for the Ironman totalled twenty-two hours weekly with early swims in Coventry, hundreds of bike miles, and then filling in with about forty miles of runs weekly—how did I do it? It was like a full-time job. Nevertheless, I still finished the year with the St. Albans marathon in 3.17 my 35th marathon. I was also running for the Massey Ferguson Club just down the road, in road races and cross-country league matches so was pretty fit. During that time in my fifty-fourth year, I also won quite a few trophies for O/50 events for my club and in open races the pick of which was to win the Massey 5 vets in 28: 43. i.e. 5: 45 minute miling! Later when I was 60+ with Graham Patton and Alan Oglesby my fellow Massey runners surprised ourselves by winning Gold in the UK 10k relay race.

My first Ironman ultra-marathon with medal,
bike and pancake pan (for the marathon leg!) at Ironbridge,
Shropshire in a time of 13: 34: Missed a Hawaii
place by 30 seconds! 1991.

My World Triathlon Dream Debut Shattered

My times in the various Olympic distance triathlons (1 mile swim, 25 miles bike, and 6.2 mile run) were good enough to qualify me for the World Triathlon Championships (age section) in Toronto, Canada in 1992. Unfortunately, I was destined never to compete in Canada for a very good reason. With only two weeks to go with my training going really well in all three disciplines, disaster struck. I was returning from a fifty mile training bike ride around Warwickshire when I skidded on a diesel slick on a roundabout in Kenilworth. The bike slid from under me, and I landed heavily on my right side. I quickly realised my leg was not in good shape when I tried to crawl to the curb, my bike still in the middle of the road. Eventually, someone rescued the bike, and just minutes later, a car with two young ladies stopped and asked me if I was all right. Silly question really! Amazingly, they were nurses on their way to Coventry & Warwickshire Hospital for their afternoon shift. What luck—serendipity! Someone up there really did like me! In the twenty-five minute ride to Coventry, my leg felt every twist and road indentation, but once there, I was whisked into X ray where it was confirmed I had suffered a clean fracture of the main fibula—a broken leg, so no World Champs for me! So, 1992 was going to be a memorable year for all the wrong reasons.

'It's an ill wind that blows no-one any good' goes the saying, and sure enough the 'ill wind' that blew in the form of the broken leg lead to my taking up the tenor saxophone again after ten years gathering dust. With the aid of a first class tutor, I studied hard for Grades through the Guildhall School of Music (jazz syllabus) and eventually reached the top grade 8, not without sweating in the exams rooms along the way in Coventry Cathedral. During this time, a repair to my tenor introduced me to the leader of the North Warwickshire Jazz Orchestra in Nuneaton, and it wasn't long before I was playing second tenor and doing gigs in the area. Subsequently, I moved to a nearer orchestra in Solihull, The Skyliners, to play my newly acquired alto sax, playing the baritone sax part. This along with my clarinet is still an important part of my musical life.

Blowin Tenor Sax in the NWJO (North Warwickshire Jazz Orchestra). 2ne from right. Nuneaton. Warks. 1995

Guildhall School of Music and Drama

CERTIFICATE OF ACHIEVEMENT

DALE LYONS
HAS PASSED
THE GRADE 8 EXAMINATION
IN JAZZ SAXOPHONE

'A treasured possession', my Grade 8 Tenor Saxophone certificate. Guildhall School of Music—1996

Memorable Runs Around The World

The 89 marathons I have completed so far to April 2011 include the marathons in two Ironman events. This Ultra event has three sections: a 2.4 miles swim, a 112 mile bike, and a 26.2 mile run. I have completed the New York seven times since 1981 the last in 2004; a charity relay run for Macmillan Nurses across America, which involved me running 209 miles in twelve days, tossing pancakes from Washington to San Francisco; the Centenary Boston Marathon in 1995 with 42,000 runners; the Berlin Marathon in 1987 (before the wall came down); the Swiss Mountain marathon in Davos a 43-mile race, tossing a pancake in 10: 57; the toughest in the UK being the Snowdon Marathon in 1984 again tossing pancakes in 3: 29; and, of course, my fastest marathon in 2: 57: 15 in Wolverhampton. My fastest London in 1986 was tossing a pancake in 3: 06. One of my other claims to fame is to have run five more London Marathons than anyone else having run a double three times and three times on the same day making thirty-six to date. Up to 2011, there were only eighteen runners left who had completed every London Marathon, the fastest by far is Chris Finill, a Guinness record holder who has run every one in under 3 hours—some feet!.

Resting in Utah on the Trans. American relay charity run sponsoring Macmillan Nurses. Note the record braking pancake pan which I used to toss all my 207 miles. September 1993.

My Guinness world record egg & spoon marathon
(guinea fowl) in 3:43. With Harry Carpenter Muscular
Dystrophy charity team captain helping and Matthew Kelly
(top actor & TV star) in attendance 1990

Guinness World Records in The London Marathon

Apart from the world record pancake toss in the London in 1982 and 1986, I have set Guinness records for the fastest Egg & Spoon Marathon in 1991 in 3: 43 and a three-legged marathon with Dave Pettifer in 1995 in 3: 58. At the moment the Egg & Spoon record still stands! In 1992 after breaking my leg training for the World Triathlon championships, I took up wheel-chair racing and completed a number of events in order to keep fit. The Chelmsley 10 k, the Clowne half marathon, which I won—as the only wheelchair to finish; and the Great North Run in 1992 in 3.13 and last wheelchair! Finally, in October 1992, I completed the Abingdon Marathon (wheelchair section) and came third, much to the surprise of the permanently disabled competitors! Three month before, I had completed the European Ironman in Roth in 11: 35 over an hour faster than my first Ironman in Ironbridge. I was the first UK athlete over fifty but still missed out on a Hawaii place by over sixty minutes—tough field!

On my way over Tower Bridge in the 6th London Marathon to a World pancake record of 3:06: 'Note the pancake in mid-toss!' 1986.

A historical note on the Ironman, one of the toughest ultra-marathon challenges! This race was originally dreamt up by three athletes in Hawaii who individually, competed in three very tough races—a 2.4 mile sea swim, a bike ride of 112 miles, and a 26.2 footrace. They decided to organise the toughest race in the world by combining all three races into one annual event, thereafter called The Ironman. This event is now run in many countries around the world with the present record under eight hours! The Hawaii Ironman is the pinnacle of ultra triathlons, and entry is only through international qualifying events.

I have also completed a number of triathlons mostly at the Olympic distance. In my second Jersey Triathlon in 1991, Veronica Seyers, my Jersey triathlon friend, told me there was a magnificent trophy for the vets category (over fifty) that year with the committee chairman expecting to win it as he had the previous year. In the race itself, his swim time tied with me, but then he moved ahead in the bike section. However, the 10 k run was my forte, and with a couple of miles to go, I realised he was just a minute ahead, so I pulled out the stops, and passed him with a mile to go winning by two minutes in 2: 30! Although he was rather miffed when I received the enormous engraved silver trophy, he did have the grace to congratulate me on my win.

Finishing the London marathon for a Guinness World Record (longest egg & spoon run of 29 miles). The egg was signed by Chris Brasher founder of the London Marathon. April 1990.

Guinness 3 legged World record with Dave Pettifer 3:58:33.
in the London Marathon 1995.

Finishing the triple London (78.6 miles in 17:12:) at
61 years complete with broken wrist in sling. April 1998.

Three champions. Sandwiched between Steve Jones & Mike Gratton London Marathon winners in the '80's at a press launch before the 1985 Marathon.

With Jasper (Carrot) top midlands comedian who loaned me his hotel room for a refresher in the London Triple attempt. Blackheath 1997.

Dale's Second Chance for the World Triathlon Championship

The 1993 World Triathlon Championships were held in Manchester, and I had qualified in the over 50s age-related category with a fast time of 2.28.48 in a local Leicestershire triathlon. In the race I had a good start on the swim, but the bike course was a nightmare with a wet slick road and a tough, tricky downhill section near the start. This downhill and bend claimed quite a few of the top male and female bikers. At that time drafting (following too close|) was forbidden, and if caught, you were obliged to stop, lift the bike over your head, and remount, losing valuable seconds. I really struggled in the wet and had a poor transition into the 10 k run section eventually ending up thirteenth overall in my age group in a relatively poor time for me of 2:34:19. After the race, it was back tutoring at the O. U. summer school at York University for the remainder of the week. In Manchester, I had stayed with my son-in-law Bob's (Longworth) relations on the Saturday evening and they gave me a grand time.

Veronica Seyers a gifted athlete, triathloner and OU graduate who introduced me to the Jersey Triathlon. 1993.

On the bike section winning the Jersey triathlon vets by 3 mins. (age 55). Storms nearly cancelled the race. Channel Islands 1992.

The London Marathon Triples 1997 & 1978

My next race was training for my London Marathon Triple attempt. I entered my longest run ever, a twenty-four hour race at the North Solihull Sports Centre in Chelmsley Wood in 1997. I ran for nineteen hours, completing seventy-nine miles before an enormous foot blister put an end to my race. Despite this disappointment, the resulting stamina gain really helped to provide a solid base for my attempt at the triple. I eventually completed the triple in 1998 at the second time of asking in 17: 12 starting at 10 p.m. on the Saturday night and finishing in the Sunday main event late afternoon with splits of 5: 14, 5:23, and 6: 35, accompanied part of the way by Iona and Dick. But, no Guinness Record this time because after three months deliberation, the committee decided *'yes, the triple London is worthy of inclusion, but you have not done it fast enough'!* They were comparing my time to 100 k races running around a 400 metres track for hours whereas I had run through London streets, through the night with no maps, getting lost and with a broken wrist from snowboarding only two weeks earlier! Unfair! Unfair!

Record Keeping—A Key to Success

Part of my training involves a detailed record keeping of my runs and races which I think has been a key ingredient to my development. So, three years ago, I decided to find out how many miles I had run in training and races since getting the running bug back in 1979 some thirty-two years earlier. Back then after joining the Centurion Joggers, I embarked on the Adidas sponsored National Jogging Association (NJA) initiative to get the nation fitter. Free of charge, they issued JogLogs to record joggers' progress and awarded badges for blocks of jogging hours with the eventual Super Jogger Award for completing 250 hours. Naturally, I became a Super Jogger in record time and sported the special badge with some pride! In fact, I still have the running top sporting all the NJA jogging badges—but never wear it now. Since then, I have kept a record of every race and training run, even though the NJA is now a distant memory. Over a period of months, I added up the miles and races in each of the Joglogs, now up to 21 editions and arrived at a total milage of 40,404 up to 16 January 2011! Is that about twice around the World? Included in that mileage is 419 races made up of 89 marathons; 57 half marathons; 86—5 mile/ 5 kms;. 43—10 mile; 22—20 & 21 miles; 12 triathlons; 3 Karimor Mountain Marathons; and a host of other assorted distances. I would recommend record keeping to any athlete in any sport as it has given me four main benefits.

1. Motivation to run because you can easily plot your progress.
2. Feedback on performance to track good and poor training schedules.
3. A sense of achievement by building on your strengths and overcoming your weaknesses.
4. A historical perspective that serves as a detailed record to check on ones suspect recall.

And, of course, records can be a useful tool for analysing your declining performances over the years, as I have found to my dismay!

CERTIFICATE

The fastest pancake tossing marathon was achieved by Dale Lyons (UK) in 3 hours and 9 minutes in the 1982 London Marathon

My first Guinness World Record for the marathon pancake toss—London Marathon April 1982

A New Bionic Knee Keeps Me Running

Three years ago in June 2009, a failed keyhole operation lead to a whole knee replacement with a PFC Sigma Fixed Bearing System made of titanium and plastic. After six months rehabilitation, I was able to resume training but strongly advised running was not recommended. So I took up speed walking and have since 'walked' six marathons: one on crutches and a few shorter races. So far the knee is still in good shape.

So how long will I be able to keep 'running'? I suppose as long as my body can keep up to the mark with the help perhaps of the amazing advances in replacement surgery. Certainly my motivation to run or in my case speed-walk is as keen as ever. Now at seventy-four years of age, I guess that time is getting ever closer to hanging up my trainers!

The 30th London Marathon 'EVERPRESENTS'
a diminishing breed of #18. April 2010.

Wheelchair racing after breaking my leg——training for the
Great North Run——1992

Chapter 14

Rugby & Rotary Experiences, 2000-2008

Finding a New Home in a Village—Church Lawford Warwickshire

Initially, my search for a new page and home in my life had taken me all over the West & East Midlands, looking for the ideal property. I wanted an older property in a rural setting if possible around the £120/150 k mark. My initial forays into Leamington/Kenilworth found them too expensive and unsuitable. Another attractive area nearer Birmingham was Water Orton and Coleshill but a new Motorway threat loomed, the Birmingham Toll Road so they were ruled out too. I was forced to widen my search area into the East Midlands, and eventually my search ended with 8 Smithy Lane, Church Lawford a sweet little terraced cottage in a cul-de-sac of eight houses near Rudgby. It ticked all the boxes.

A New Partner via Rugby Rotary

So after the split with Angela, I was happy to be on my own with just Smudger and Sooty for company, and so quickly settled down into village life with great neighbours and a great pub the Old Smithy. Prior to leaving Meriden, I had made enquiries about joining a Rotary Club, and so once in Church Lawford, I found out that the current president of Rugby Rotary,

Bruce Gould, lived in the village. Two weeks later, he invited me to their annual charity ball in Rugby, and it was there that I met Janet Tomlinson who had been divorced about three years and lived in Edgbaston. She had known Pam and Bruce many years and had reluctantly agreed to attend the Ball at which I had also been invited as Bruce's guest. Anyway we met, danced, chatted, and had a pleasant evening. After I returned from a BESO assignment in Kathmandu about a month later, I contacted Janet and after the usual 'getting-to-know' period, we settled into a lovely and loving relationship alternating between Church Lawford and Edgbaston. Bruce and Pam still deny they were matchmaking!

By 2002 and apart from house decorating, I settled into village life and getting involved in Rugby Rotary Club where I became a member and, shortly after the press & publicity officer. They were a very friendly group with about sixty members and involved in fund-raising in the area, collecting £'000s annually for all sorts of charities both at home and abroad. In 2004 I twisted a few Rotarians arms to do a charity show entitled Rotary's Got Talent. The sketches included monologues, story-telling, music and songs while I sang a Groucho number 'Lydia the Tattooed Lady' and then played 'Over the Rainbow' on my alto. We raised over £400 for Rotary charities and everyone had a delightful evenings entertainment.

Another solo event I initiated for 'Aspire' the spinal injuries charity was to 'swim the channel'. This 23 miles 'channel swim' was completed with 1,012 lengths of the local swimming baths over 4 weeks with a swim time of 17 hours 10 minutes. I raised another £500 but almost became waterlogged!

With my partner Janet (Tomlinson) happy holidaying in Normandy in 2006. We met at the Rugby Rotary Ball in 2001.

Problems of a DIY Amateur—the Refurbishment of 8 Smith Lane

No 8 was 130-year-old and in need of extensive renovation which suited my wallet as a DIY enthusiast. The previous owners, a young couple, had marginally improved the front rooms with exposed beams but had then decided to part company. Fortunately, the disgusting state of the kitchen and bathroom had put most potential buyers off, so I was able to buy the property for £117,000, which was a good deal for a property with lots of potential. Twelve months later with the aid of a jobbing Irish builder and a former runner with Centurions who was also a professional plumber, I had completely enlarged and redesigned the kitchen, knocked down a lean-to and installed a large bathroom with a bidet and a new tiled roof. Double glazed windows all round in the kitchen and bathroom completed the first stage.

Outside the kitchen was another lean-to masquerading as a mini-conservatory, which when knocked down had newspaper insulation dated 1954! A local conservatory company gave me a fantastic price, which could not have made them much profit as they had to replace a faulty wall. The new conservatory was South facing but with a four ply insulated roof, and double glazing was still comfortable even in high summer. And the quarry style stone floor I installed gave a real professional touch to the conservatory which then had access to a paved patio area and the back garden.

Finishing the Job and Learning to Cope

Over the next year, a number of in-door improvements were made starting with the lounge fireplace which was replaced with a magnificent coal gas fire and a wood and marble fireplace surround. All the gloss painted doors were removed, shipped to Coventry, stripped down to their original wood and then sealed and fitted with original brass knobs and catches to finish. I was very proud of these. My jobbing builder then did two marvellous renovations upstairs with my help. First was the installation of a new gas Combi boiler in the guest bedroom by removing the old water tanks and a linen cupboard. These two small spaces allowed the installation of a small toilet, wash basin, and in the adjacent cupboard a state-of-the-art shower cubicle. My idea of two glass bricks fitted into the outside walls of both these areas gave enough natural lighting to eliminate the need for extra lighting. New radiators were fitted into the kitchen and dining rooms as part of the central heating renovation. Throughout the kitchen and bathroom areas the electrical system was also rewired then new floors of interlocking veneered boards were installed in the bathroom and dining / music rooms—a tricky job until I got the hang of it. A final brainwave was the installation of a 6' double glazed picture window in the main bedroom facing out over the garden with stunning views of village fields, cows, sheep and the village church. Unfortunately, the first one cracked in the very last moment of fitting. Never mind, I still used it as a window in the refurbished garden shed! The main bedroom was now transformed!

Twelve months later, I completely redesigned the garden with a fish pond, rockery and stepped waterfall fountain to complete the work. Before long, frogs, newts and small water snakes had taken up residence. I was even donated an enormous golden koi which had outgrown a neighbours pond. The heavy work was done by my running friend Graham (Patten) who was glad of the extra untaxed income. The final *piece de resistance* was installing a sauna, which I had been drooling over and planning since I moved in. A small concreted area to the side of the bathroom was fitted with a beautiful pinewood designer sauna installed by Dick and myself over a long weekend. It had room for four, heated by an 8 kw stove and proved an ideal antidote to long winter runs. My home was just about complete!

Back into a Jazz Group

During one of my visits to a local working men's club in the nearby village of Brinklow, I met a musician called Bernard who had a jazz group and asked me to join having heard I played the saxophone and clarinet. I had missed playing in the Skyliners Big Band after I left Meriden and was pleased to get involved on a weekly basis with occasional gigs in the area. Also in the band was a talented guitar and banjo player, Adrian (Hirons) who offered to teach me bluegrass banjo, which I had really taken to. He even loaned me a banjo and gave me bi-weekly lessons until I was sure of the commitment. I am still playing, and he says improving after 100 lessons.

During this time, I was tempted by the Church Lawford Parish committee and Church elders to help the restoration fund by agreeing to play in a church concert on my alto sax. I duly agreed and naturally I played my favourite 'Over the Rainbow' to a sold out church. Of course, I was not the only performer on the night, and the concert raised many hundreds of pounds for the church's restoration fund. The vicar just wished he could get this congregation every Sunday!

Running with the Rugby Jolly Joggers

But where to run? Once settled, I contacted the local running club Rugby & Northampton A. C. to find they had initiated an itinerant group of hardy runners call the Jolly Joggers (JJ). Rain or shine, freezing or blisteringly hot the JJ would meet every Sunday at 8 a.m. for a two-hour x-country slog. Each run would be organised by the person living in the chosen spot around Rugby. Snacks and drinks were usually organised by the lady runners and consumed at the end of the two hour run after which next week's location was agreed. Smithy Lane was a popular meeting venue as the post-run catering was superior! Twice annually, we had a breakfast run meeting with a 'full monty' at the 'Hungry Sausage' on the A45 south of Rugby with up to thirty runners. This was a big miss when I moved to Birmingham in 2008.

Smudger Lyons a long hair Coventry farm cat with a lovely personality. Still with me 19 years old!

Two Deaths at Smithy Lane

Keeping me company at 8 Smith Lane was Sooty and Smudger. Sooty was then about twenty years old, became frail and contacted inoperable cancer. When he was put to sleep at Furber's vets, I cried buckets as he looked at me and then closed his eyes—I'm welling up now just typing this! To keep Smudger's company, I went to the local farm and 'bought' Scamp, a feisty marmalade kitten, who terrorised the neighbour's dog. Sadly, only eight months later, he contracted some incurable disease and was put to sleep—again more buckets. Both were given appropriate monuments in my Smithy Lane garden attended by Smudger.

By this time, I had been released by Coventry University in a swingeing cut of part-time lecturers. I had, however, taken up another lecturing appointment at Warwickshire College in Leamington and Morton Morrell. The lectures at Morton were to HND students in Equine Studies with human resource management. It was very hard work as these young ladies were not interested in anything but horses. Still they were neither disruptive nor inattentive, and the part-time rates in 2001 were £25 an hour and I could do all the photocopying for my consultancy work. The only downside was the thirty-six mile round trip from Rugby.

National Trust (NT) Volunteering

Rodney and Susan West, my friends from the College of Food were now in Bristol. Rodney had joined the volunteer service of the NT and encouraged me to join implying there was loads of talent and fun at minimal cost. Easily lead as I am and interested in a new challenge, I became a volunteer and for about four years went for weekends and occasional weeks all around the country, repairing dry stone walls, rebuilding fences, chopping up forests, setting fire to unwanted vegetation, digging out blocked drains and ditches, stewarding equine events, repairing pathways on the southern coastal routes and generally tidying up overgrown stately home gardens. It was hard work but very enjoyable and a really good laugh. I eventually gave it up after a really badly organised event where we were twiddling thumbs for most of the day.

BESO/ VSO Volunteering

At the same time, I was involved with the British Executive Service Overseas (BESO) which I mentioned earlier describing my China assignment. During the years 1999 to 2008, I was involved in projects in Eastern Europe, Russia, the Far East, and Africa. A summary of these assignments took in the following countries; Slovakia—helping to regenerate tourism in six spar towns after the Russians left; China (Northeast)—retraining hotel staff and management in Western hotel systems, marketing and management in Chengyang; Estonia, designing the curriculum for a catering college in Tallin; Ukraine—improving the sales, marketing, and technical skills in a hotel and leisure complex in Lviv/Lvov; Nepal—training technical staff in supervisory and technical skills and job organisation in Kathmandu and Pokara with the Shangri-La Hotel chain in two three-week assignments in 1997 and 2001 and finally; Nigeria in Lagos detailed next.

'Thanks to Dale' on VSO Management Development Assignment by Staff and Management at the Shangri-La Village, Pokara, Nepal—2001

A safari break 'training' an elephant during a VSO assignment in Pokara, Nepal for the Shangri La hotel group in Katmandu. 2001.

Lagos Nigeria—The Final VSO Assignment

In Lagos Nigeria in 2007 I was accompanied by Janet to train managers, and staff in management, technical skills, and operations in four hotels in Lagos. One of these was the Eko, Lagos' largest, with about 1,500 staff. In addition to training the hotel's general manager asked us to be mystery guests for one weekend to give him an objective assessment of both the hotel and the serviced apartments. There was so much wrong with each area that the manager might have thought we were making up the problems which were legion—we weren't! On our return, I sent in a detailed report but we never had a reply!

Management Development & Hash House Harriers in Lagos

Initially, the Palmview Manor Hotel was our base where we established a primary training centre for staff and managers. Here we trained many staff in a wide range of operational and supervisory skills such as customer care, time management, selling and cost control. Each morning on arriving for breakfast, we would be asked 'how was the night?' 'Very dark' I would reply to the amusement of the staff. In addition to the six-hour training day, I reorganised the breakfast service and retrained all the waiting staff, including the head waiter. When we left, we never heard from the owner of the Palmview Manor or had any thanks for our voluntary efforts. We vowed never to return, though we were asked by the VSO clients to do another assignment. Whilst at the Palmview, we were also promised tours to attractive areas outside of Lagos, but these never materialised. The only place that was organised for us by the clients was a visit to the Lagos yacht club, the up-market watering hole for ex-pats from the UK and other European countries. Mostly they were a sad bunch who couldn't afford to leave and had left their links back home too long ago to return.

The bright spot for us in all this was to be chauffeured everywhere, it being too dangerous for us to venture out alone (Hash House Harriers apart). Also having Janet with me was a timely bonus as it would have been a pretty boring and lonely existence without her. She did a great supervisory job with the trainees especially at the Eko hotel and sorted out most of the admin. and photocopying requirements of which there were mountains. Twice during our stay, we ate out, resulting I think in getting the dreaded trots which I eventually sorted with a bottle of kaolin and morphine.

One major problem we had at the hotel was with the failure of the main generator. Electrical power is totally unreliable in Lagos, so every hotel has to have its own generator and there was no piped gas. In temperatures at night of 34 °C, we sweated away for four nights with water being hauled to each room by the porters. Hot food was unavailable. Eventually a new generator the size of a small room was delivered and hooked up but with the loss of about half the hotel's customers. Our eventual departure was as traumatic as our arrival with personal searches of our luggage by the army at the airport so we were very, very glad to leave Nigeria and back into civilization.

A City in Decline

Unfortunately, Lagos was a city in decline, the capital having moved to Abuja 400 miles away and apparently designed on the Paris concentric model. Many people lived rough on the streets in Lagos and scratched a living by meandering through the slow moving traffic with what appeared to be reckless abandon, selling an amazing selection of consumer goods. I saw only two sets of traffic lights in this city of ten million with traffic routinely grid-locked. Anyone with money lived behind guarded, razor-wire protected houses. Briefly I joined a local Hash House Harrier group to keep up my marathon training, and they ran in 30+ °c temperature in the evening for about five miles. It was truly exhausting with the heat and traffic fumes but very entertaining due to the Harrier's quirky ceremonies, generous hospitality, and their *raison d'etre*—'never let the running interfere with the drinking'!

Lagos certainly was an experience but one that we were resolved not to repeat! This was underlined by the hotel's shoddy treatment regarding Janet's expenses and hospitality, which they expected me to pay. Eventually I contacted the local BESO representative and told him I only accepted the assignment on the understanding that Janet was an integral part of the training team. I never heard any more! This was my final BESO/VSO assignment.

Chapter 15

Back to Birmingham, 2008-2011

Moving into 'Leafy' Edgbaston

Not hearing from me after the Rotary Ball, Janet thought our brief meeting had been our last as she later told me. I do like to keep people guessing and eventually, after returning from Nepal, I got Janet's phone from Pam, Bruce's wife and we met up at Smithy Lane. After seven years back and forth from Church Lawford to Edgbaston, we decided to merge the households, and naturally I lost. So I sold up for a very good price of £250,000, just before the credit crunch bit, to a young couple and moved back to Brum, after an absence of twenty years. Edgbaston, Birmingham was my new home. My next door neighbour in Smithy Lane, Richard Grant, very generously helped me with the move in one of his company's white vans. Mind you, after disposing of most of my furniture and effects to family, friends and e bay, there wasn't a lot to move—particularly as Janet had a houseful of everything we needed. I was granted the upstairs bedroom and adjacent room for an office and en-suite so it was more than adequate, and once I'd sorted out new office furniture and a new computer things were just tikkety-boo.

The first few weeks were periods of adjustment with lively discussions and a bit of wrangling about what items of mine could clutter the general areas of the house such as the lounge, hall, and kitchen. Remember, Janet had in her new home for about ten years so having a 'lodger' took some readjustment, even if self-imposed. Eventually she accepted that I would personalise my area upstairs and make some inroads into other rooms.

My newest Granddaughter Niamh (spelled Neeve—it's Irish) at 3 years & daughter of Kyla. Sharp as a tack! 2011.

Reconnecting My Social, Sporting and Cultural Links

So what did I miss in my move from Church Lawford? My Sundays with the Jolly Joggers especially and jogs around the Warwickshire countryside—certainly! My bi-weekly visits to Rugby Rotary and the lively committees and fellowship events—absolutely! The village camaraderie and monthly meals in the hall—without doubt! The proximity of banjo tuition and the weekly jazz group! The fresh air and countryside views—oh yes! The cottage I had put so much time, effort and thought into! That was the real wrench even now after three years away.

But, on the plus side, I didn't miss the eighty mile round trip travelling to Brum and neither did Janet who did most of the travelling as I had

Smudger to consider. Smudger, in fact, seemed to settle in quite well, and there was lots of off road gardens to discover and explore, although the wildlife, rabbits especially are in short supply. Another plus was the convenience of shops, transport, and nightlife (cinemas / theatres) close at hand. We were also less than two miles from the city centre in 'leafy' Edgbaston with a direct canal footpath link nearby. I quickly sorted out other options such as French lessons, another Rotary Club, the Bournville Harriers running club, a local gym, and swimming baths in Harborne as they were all on the doorstep.

In addition, my banjo lessons eventually lead me to join the Midland Fretted Orchestra in nearby Bearwood, playing classical banjo with mandolins and guitars. We rehearse every fortnight and play a few concerts to raise funds for the orchestra's costs. So, another string had been added to my musical 'bow'.

My daughters were delighted with the move as they both had a real affection for Janet—always a plus. Janet's friends at Inner Wheel whom I knew anyway were also pleased that they could invite us as a couple to social events and dinner dates. We both rubbed along extremely well with disagreements quickly resolved and no recriminations.

Kyla and Simon's wedding in Finchley London. L to R Iona, Angela (first wife), Kyla, Simon, Myself & Janet. Bottom row L to R. Marisa, Anna & Joe my grand-kids (standing). 2005.

My first and last tandem parachute jump (from 13,000') sponsoring the QAC the local blind school and raising over £700 as a member of Edgbaston Convention Rotary club. 2011.

Problems of Adjustment in Richmond Hill Gardens

Occasionally, I would instigate a discussion on the topic 'how are we doing' as Janet was less proactive in coming out with her concerns. These had the effect of clearing the air.

It is now over three years since the move, and during that time, we have had holidays in Australia and New Zealand, Canada and Alaska, toured America's South and the length of France and had cruises in the Mediterranean, the Baltic, and Alaska. We've also had a delightful time in Lanzarote with Janet's family and a first ever river cruise up the Rhine. We've sandwiched in away weekends with my family to Whitby, Center Parcs and Feurtaventura, for the first family outing outside the UK.

Naturally, I have kept up the Marathon running even with the new right knee replacement and additionally with half marathons in Birmingham and Coventry. Hopefully, knee willing I intend to reach 100 marathons on or before 2013. With an unofficial marathon around the canals and paths in the area, I've reached the eighty-nineth! So please let the good times continue!

Chapter 16

Reminiscences of My Dad—
Joseph Robinson Lyons

Early Years in South Shields

Dad came from a tough upbringing largely without his father, who left home for the First World War as a medic and never returned. Apparently, he was a top man in setting broken limbs—quite useful during the Great War. He chose to stay away for reasons I never discovered, although there were rumours of another lady in the mix. In fact later on his mother had him imprisoned for non-payment of alimony but Dad eventually bailed him out!

Dad told me his early years with his four brothers and one sister, Autie Sadie, as the second youngest toughened him up. They lived in Dakar Street, South Shields, which is still there. At school, fighting was endemic, and abuse in the classroom by masters by the paddle and 'dusting the floor' with the pupils was the accepted means of preserving discipline. After school, Dad earned his keep by delivering groceries to the wealthy on an ancient bike after which he became a trainee in a local chemist. To keep away hunger pangs, Dad would cadge a half-penny (quarter pence in new money) for a 'slice and dip' which was a thick slice of white bread smeared with beef dripping which often sufficed for his tea.

Dad Starts a Career in the Hospitality Industry

Things took a turn for the better when he avoided the normal employment path of coal mining, ship building, or labouring to become an apprentice in Newcastle's Union Club—a bastion for the movers and shakers of the North East's industrial might with mine owners, ship building magnates, Vickers engineering owners, bankers, and top men from the business community. This was another world for Dad, which he embraced with come enthusiasm as a junior steward. Culinary and service standards were of the first order with training, discipline and long and hard hours to match. At least, he had a roof over his head, a very smart uniform, regular meals and pocket money, in effect, luxury by his previous living standards. It was here that he met my Mother Mary Josephine Tearse, a senior housekeeper at the Club and two years older than Dad.

This quality training eventually lead him to London as a top waiter with co-incidentally the J Lyons Corner House and the Great Western Hotel and in the summer months, to Blackpool (Tower Ballroom), St. Ann's on Sea (Majestic hotel), and Harrogate (Three Arrows Hotel). The County Hotel Carlisle was Dad's last stop before the Rex Hotel Whitley Bay, where he became Head Waiter at the best hotel in the North East.

Living On Your Wits in the Depression

During the 20s depression when working at the County Hotel, he had problems with his teeth, and the dentist convinced him that in the long run, it would be better if he had *all* his teeth out and dentures fitted—amazing! Immediately after the total extraction, he biked all the way back from North Shields to Carlisle and was working the next day—unbelievable but true. During this time, he sought jobs away from depressed Tyneside during the 1920s and 1930s by riding various brands of motorbikes among which was a Brough Superior. And once, before his biking days, he even took a freighter from the Tyne to London to save money. The journey took twenty-four hours!

J. Lyons & Co—The Ultimate Tough Organisation

His first job for J. Lyons had a curious start because when asked for his name at Personnel and he said Joseph Lyons they said 'no, no that's the name of the company'. After he repeated it was also *his* name they decided to avoid confusion and in a nod to his Irish roots he was thereafter called Pat by the restaurant supervisor. As a station waiter at the Tottenham Court Road Corner House, he was paid the princely sum of ten shillings a week with one minutes notice on either side! This 50 p in new money was spirited away to get service from the various departments he had to rely on for service such as the still room and kitchen. In other words, his 'wages' were made up by customers' tips and nothing else—unless he could work a good fiddle. This practice however was fraught with the risk of terminal employment if caught and no reference for future work.

However, Dad was not without guile and used a very simple but effective 'fiddle' to bolster his income. Using this fiddle sparingly, he would list the items and amounts on the bill accurately but then add up the total incorrectly by say two shillings (10 p) or ½ crown (12.5 p). Rarely would this error be spotted, but if it was Dad would instantly own up and offer to return the money before any supervisor noticed. Invariably, the customer would decline saying 'that's all right, keep the money'.

The Lyons' food control system was foolproof by ensuring the company never lost out to any illicit transactions. Waiters were given a float and had to 'buy' their food with tickets bought from the cashier with their float. They then presented these to the kitchen for the items on their order and, at the end of the day the float was returned, and any residue was theirs. If they missed items off the bill, then they were the losers and not J. Lyons.

A more difficult scam was used at tea time whereby uneaten cakes were secreted to be sold later. Spare cups were hooked under tables for the same reason. For example, waiters could then make up a tea without 'buying' tickets for these cakes and cups. So for a party of say four customers, they would only order three teas, pocketing the surplus amounts for one tea.

Making Money at The Seaside

During the Summer season, Dad would work the seaside resorts as tips and work were plentiful especially at the Tower Ballroom in Blackpool. The work was hard, and for the whole of their shift, the restaurants were packed with queues around the block. Dad told me that many waiters had travelled from depressed areas of Wales and were under-nourished and unfit for the taxing work. He said that in one season, he attended ten funerals which worked out to about 10 % of the waiting staff! One scam at the Tower went disastrously wrong, but fortunately Dad would have nothing to do with it. Similar to the J. Lyons control system, waiters had to buy tickets for food and drink, presenting them to either bars or kitchen for the amount required. A group of waiters decided to by-pass the restaurant ticket system by buying rolls of the same tickets from a printer in Blackburn. They then distributed the counterfeit tickets to their group who then proceeded straight to bars and kitchens for service bi-passing the cashiers. On the first day of the scam, the restaurant was packed with customers, and it didn't take long for the bored cashiers to realise that something was badly wrong and called the supervisors.

The restaurant was closed immediately. Customers were ushered out without paying for their food, and the local police were called in. The culprit's lockers were opened, and the illegal rolls of tickets taken as evidence. The guilty waiters were summarily dismissed and blackballed from all the Tower companies and would find it very hard to get any similar work that season! Dad thought it was an audacious scam with potential but implemented too quickly.

Dad also worked at the luxurious Majestic Hotel at St. Annes on Sea close to Blackpool and told me one story that shows that autocratic management has its limitations. In the first week of his employment in the still room (where the crockery & cutlery was collected), a waiter with a tray of glasses allowed them to slide off the tray, breaking every one. 'Oh dear,' he said, 'there's my sixpence gone again'. It transpired that all the waiting staff were docked sixpence (2.5 p), a week by management for breakages. Certainly sixpence would not have covered the cost of these breakages!

The worst stations in a restaurant, especially at J. Lyons corner house, were the ones in the centre of the room, known affectionately as 'spike island'. They were the last to be occupied and the last to be vacated, thereby minimising waiter's tips, which was their sole source of income. On this station, waiters had to work extra time on customer's reluctant to leave so they would lobby supervisors to be allocated wall stations.

A Top Job Beckons in Whitley Bay

Eventually Dad found the ideal position, Head Waiter or *Maitre d'Hotel* at the Rex Hotel in the early thirties. This lasted until his disastrous motor-cycle accident on the day before World War II broke out. Many of the hotel's clients were the *creme de la creme* from the North East as well the top football teams from the first Division (now Premiership) who stayed prior to playing Newcastle United. I still have a collection of autographs of the top teams that Dad's job enabled him to obtain. Also, being a family man, he gave employment in the dining room to some of his brothers who were either unemployed or on hard times. Unfortunately, some of them played the family loyalty card and let him and the hotel down so he had no option but to dismiss them on occasions.

In the Rex job, Dad had moved into management so the poacher had now become gamekeeper as he knew all the tricks and fiddles of the trade, with the result that neither staff nor management rarely upstaged him. He was firm but fair in all his dealings and introduced a tronc (tip box system) that rewarded staff in relation to their service and position, excluding him as management.

After losing his leg in 1939, he eventually returned to management with part ownership of the Cliff Hotel in 1948 and made a great success of it (reported in Chapter 2). After Mum died in 1953, he travelled around the Country doing catering and chefs work in many good hotels and restaurants. These included the Park Hotel in Tynemouth as aboyer (quality controller on meal output), at the Bell Inn in Wark Northumberland as head chef and as a catering manager (Burser/Chef) at the prestigious St. Bees public boys school on the North West Coast of Cumbria. The 100 odd boys were routinely allocated to kitchen chores, and Dad told me on one occasion at breakfast, the head boy came to him with a request for three and four minute boiled eggs. Instead of giving the boy short shrift with what was in effect a ludicrous request with 100 boiled eggs to cook, Dad said 'certainly', and would he (head boy) just write in pencil on the each egg the minutes that each boy required then everyone would be happy! Needless to say *everyone* got the same number of minutes, and if anyone complained their egg was too hard or soft, who got the blame? The head boy, of course, not Dad—sorted!

A cartoon of Dad age 32 when Head Waiter at the prestigious Rex Hotel in Whitley Bay,. drawn by the noted illustrator Dudley Hallwood with members of the management team. 1935.

Joseph Robinson Lyons Retires After Sixty Years in Catering

Dad eventually came home to work at the Park Hotel in Tynemouth, a beautiful art deco-style building overlooking the longsands and North Sea. Despite his lack of mobility, he ran the service hotplate as a quality controller for eight years, and God help the chefs whose meals didn't meet his rigorous quality standards! He finally retired from the Park in his late seventies to put his single foot up at 4 Exeter Road, North Shields, his home for forty years.

How do you sum up JRL as a father? He had high standards both at work and home and lead by example. A disciplinarian? Yes! But fair, and I was never physically punished. His bark was worse than his bite! He rarely involved himself in my sporting interests however such as football, although I believe he took great pride in my achievements both in my career and in sports. He never gave me a cuddle, but he was sociable, was well-liked and respected wherever he went! He had a great sense of humour and loved Laurel & Hardy and slapstick comedy. My daughters were very fond of him and he would always entertain them for hours.

Above all, he was resolute and made me believe in a worthwhile career. For these reasons and many more, he was a great role model as a father and family man. On many occasions, I hear myself using expressions he used and think to myself *'he is still part of my life'*. He died age ninety-three in 1995, while I was in China on assignment and was buried in the same grave at Mum in North Shield's Preston Cemetery near to Granny Tearse. Apart from the family and some care workers, few attended the funeral as most of Dad's friends and work colleagues had pre-deceased him! I gave him a heart felt oration during the service and really felt his spirit was with me at that time.

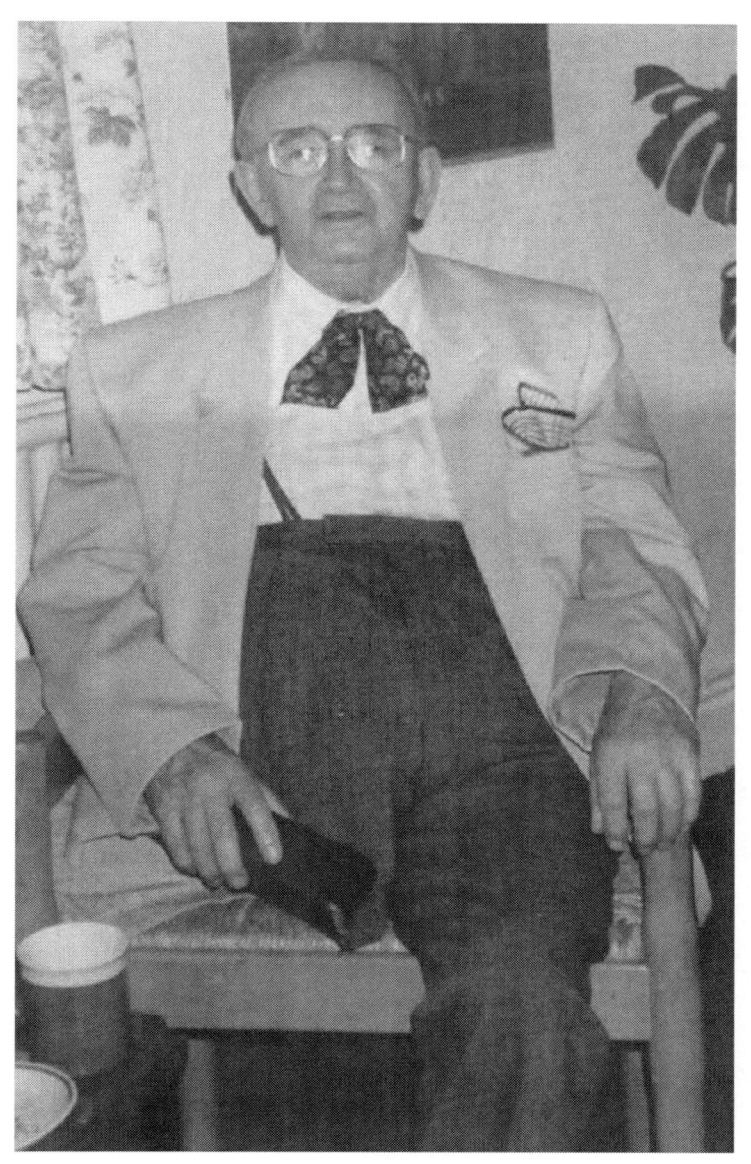

Joseph Robinson Lyons (Dad) at 90! 'Looking Good!'—1993

Chapter 17

Final Thoughts

My lovely family with Anna, Joe, Iona, Kyla & Marisa behind me & Janet. 2006.

Why Write an Autobiography?

I started this autobiography as a two-year project. Now, over three years on I feel hopeful I have covered many of the memorable events of my life, if not most. In fact, in the past few months, there have been memories dredged up I haven't covered but which might have made interesting reading. But what the hell, most if not all autobiographies are incomplete by their very nature, relying on fallible and often failing memories for situations and events long gone.

Who is Dale Robinson Lyons?

So what kind of person am I? What makes me tick? I suppose it depends on who you ask as everyone has a different take on others, depending on their experiences and relationships. Some of my employees have said I was a stickler and a disciplinarian but fair and sociable. My bosses would say I am zealous, trustworthy, reliable, and good at the job whether operationally or in management but rather obsessive. Others that I was impulsive and thoughtless. My daughters consider me helpful, considerate, and sensitive with a sharp sense of humour perhaps based on my adoration of Laurel and Hardy. They also think I am short-tempered, forgetful, and demanding.

My friends have called me adventurous with a short attention span, which reflects I suppose an extrovert personality. I certainly have to be doing things and am certainly achievement oriented perhaps to a fault. Witness that *all* my qualifications have been achieved on a part-time basis, including my master's degree. Some of my partners have seen traces of liberality and anti-chauvinism in my behaviour—I insisted that Sue, my second wife kept her maiden name. I certainly love animals of all kinds, especially cats, and sports of all kinds many of which I have tried—rugby being the exception. My daughters would say I have a live-and-let-live attitude to most people, although I do not suffer fools gladly. I probably make more enemies than friends and find it difficult to turn the other cheek. I am a social animal at heart but find a quiet contentment in my own company.

Am I an optimist? Well, I do believe in the axiom *'there is always a parking place'* (usually near the entrance!)

There you have it—make up your own mind.

Who are My Role Models?

But who are my role models? In sport, definitely Lance Armstrong coming back from 'terminal' cancer to win seven Tour de Frances. Football my favourite sport has to include Bobby Moore and another Geordie Bobby

Charlton with the wizard Georgie Best one of the greats. My cinema idols would have to include Clint Eastwood for his anti-authority no-nonsense demeanour in the Dirty Harry films and 'Humph' (Humphrey Bogart) and Cagney, although as a film buff I could name dozens more. One of my favourite politicians would be Bill Clinton, the 'comeback kid,' for despite all his wayward behaviour he made a positive contribution. Tommy Cooper would be my favourite comedian for real belly laughs, closely followed by 'the little tramp' Chaplin for his brand of roughhouse sadistic slapstick. L & H are in there, of course as are the Marx Brothers with Groucho my favourite with expressions such as 'I've had a lovely evening, but this wasn't it'! and 'whatever it is, I'm against it!' In jazz the lyrical saxophonist Paul Desmond of 'Take Five' fame coupled with the quintessential Dave Bruckbeck would be my jazz musician favourites but Bird (Charlie Parker), Dizzy and Miles (Davis), the be-bop and 'cool' jazz founders are just as central.

However, I do detest soaps, most fatuous reality shows, and cannot abide quiz shows of any kind as a filler for decent TV. Give me a well-made documentary and a re-run of Dad's Army or Hi-de-Hi any time.

As reading is one of my greatest pleasures, I do have a liking for the classics and most crime writers are a regular pleasure although I will enjoy any well written novel or biography. Entertaining popular writers too I will scour my local library for. But my early years were enhanced by Rupert, Bunter, The Hotspur, The Rover, and Just William, which I still dip into and encourage my grand-children to read by trickling them favourite books from time to time. Frank Sinatra has to be my favourite singer, although Tony Bennett in his prime must come a close second. The theatre is also a great enjoyment, but there are far too many shows to single out, although Mel Brooks' *The Producers*, *The Music Man*, and *Guys and Dolls* are three of my favourites. In films, there are too many but Bill Murray in *'Groundhog Day'* is a perennial favourite and of course, Westerns will always be a target, like the *'Magnificent Seven'*. Finally I will go a long way to hear a favourite classical concert piece although with Symphony Hall on the doorstep it isn't that far!

Earlier reference was made to my chess interests at school, and these lead to a thriving and long-lasting love affair in making and collecting chess sets. At one time, I had over fifty sets ranging from 19c Cantonese Ivory to modern sets of unique brass, crystal, Kenyan malachite and ivory, and ones I made out of copper, old pre-decimal coins, old Daily Mail machine parts.

A Disney Animals set was made with Plaster of Paris moulds and coloured with the help of my daughters when they were 6 and 8 years old.

A selection of my Chess Sets—Some made, some bought—(ivory, malachite, brass, chrystal)

Visiting the only Laurel and Hardy museum in Ulverston,
Cumbria where Stan was born on June 16th 1890.
His house is still lived in. 1989.

Who Should Be The Beneficiaries?

This autobiography has been written primarily for my family, that is my daughters, grandchildren, my partner Janet and family, and close friends, but maybe those also who have an interest in the recollections of someone raised in the North East during difficult and sometimes dangerous economic and social times.

It has also been written for me as an attempt to answer the question posed in the title, A Search for Recognition. Whether this autobiography has done that is for readers to consider.

Overall, it is a factual rather than a speculative account of my life and times and perhaps a little too detailed at times with my marathons for example. However, marathons and running have taken up an important slice of my mature years and are still an abiding interest so please allow me this indulgence.

In this respect, I think you will find the marathon reports in the appendices light hearted reminiscences and tongue in cheek recollections.

If, in the reading you find any errors, duplications, verbosity, inaccuracies and any lack of clarity I hope you will bear in mind that this is my first publication.

Overall, I have tried to be entertaining with as lively and humorous account of events as my linguistic shortcomings will allow. Hopefully, some of my readers will agree with this sentiment.

Appendix 1

My Daughters' Memories

Memories of my Father—Kyla Lyons

I have one image of you and mum together: mum sitting on your lap with you on the loo and both of you smiling and happy. As I write this, I wonder what you were up to!

I remember all the animals we had in the house alive and stuffed! The myna birds and the gerbils and the untimely accidental drowning (gerbil) in the toilet!

I have memories of you being at 4 Beverley when the brook flooded and came up to our back step and Iona crying on bonfire night, because you had shaved off your beard. I again have a recollection of being at the top of the stairs with Iona and crying but not sure why! I know I had happy times with you modelling the animal chess pieces and painting them, also having to sit still when you sculptured my profile.

I can recall feeling so excited when we went to Middlesex Polytechnic Christmas parties, as they held a magical quality for me, especially sitting on the steam train riding around the corridors.

I remember finding bird's eggs and hiding them in my knickers. I do remember the holiday when we all went to in the French Alps near Grenoble in the open-air swimming pool, even though it was misty and cold outside. Another time where we had gone down to the shore, and locals started shouting to move away as the tide was rapidly rising.

The Christmas at 4 Beverley Avenue when I got a dollhouse from Father Christmas and being so thrilled. We also had the stilts you made for many years, and I can still recall walking on them in the street.

I have magical memories of visiting your sister at the old post office and our holidays at the National Trust houses. One Christmas, in particular, where John (Flint) and Bernard and Dad were all playing instruments and the other adults singing on New Year's Eve. I came down stairs and loved the atmosphere, feeling very happy to be part of such joy!

I don't really have memories of when you left home but know I missed you and felt in the minority in our home. Looking back, I think mum and I were and are quite similar and could really wind each other up. You somehow balanced this out, and when growing up, I always saw you as my ally. I don't think I talked much to you or Mum about this but have memories of telling my junior teacher about how much I missed you.

You were portrayed as unthinking, selfish, and self-centred by Mum and your sister. I know we all have these qualities to varying degrees, but your positive attributes were not mentioned, and this is what I grew up with. You were my Dad, and I loved you, so these contradictions were rather confusing.

Once you had moved out of 4 Beverley, you were still very much part of my life. I have clear memories of swimming with you and Iona every Tuesday and choosing whatever we liked in the vending machines. There was one occasion when you bought my summer shoes. I was in junior school and was so excited to have got sandals with a heel instead of our usual Clarks shoes. Then, they were not the fashion items they are today. I had simple tastes and interests and remember being in the school playground mesmerised by their beauty. Unfortunately, they did not last long, but I loved them.

Once you moved to Birmingham, I enjoyed lots of visits to Birmingham College of Food and being fascinated with those crazy (paternoster) lifts and eating well-presented and tasty food in the restaurant and looking forward to the dessert trolley.

I also remember feeling a lot of guilt! Guilt if we did not participate in the Sunday Times National Fun Run; guilt if I was not supporting you in the London Marathon; guilt for not being the daughter you would have liked me to be; guilt that you paid me more attention than Iona, and having a feeling that I was unimportant! I can recall one beautiful autumnal day running in Hyde Park and not telling you it was my birthday when you hadn't remembered.

There was a definite expectation to make things special for your birthday when we visited you in Birmingham. I have some great memories of going to the London Marathon and working out how we could meet you at particular points and anticipating seeing you on route. I look back and am really glad I ran those races (London Marathon & Sunday Times Fun Runs). They are events in my life that I do remember clearly.

I did not realize until later how important a part your best friend Patrick (Churcher) played in my life. Once you moved to Birmingham, we would still stay over at his place with you. He was the only adult who would drop in unannounced at 4 Beverley for a cup of tea and felt completely accepted for who I was by him. I often think of him and wish he had met Simon and our children. I still miss him (Pat Churcher was murdered in a pub brawl in 1988).

I also have lots of good memories of my time with Jo and Dick (Delisle). I especially loved time with Jo (Delisle) and felt relaxed and at ease in her company and also later on with Phil and Mina (Thompson) your best friends.

You had a great group of friends who were good role models for me, warm, caring, interesting, and fun, and who all seemed to take Iona and I in as an extended family.

You gave me a love of Jazz music, not that I know much about it, but I love hearing the saxophone and imagine you may have played it while Mum was pregnant with me and also when we were growing up.

As an adult looking back, I realize how privileged Iona and I were to have gone skiing the number of times with you and again being surrounded by your friends. I am rather a cautions person, and so your attitude 'you can do it' (skiing) was often challenging, especially when you described the runs in far simpler terms than they were. However as an adult I appreciate this as I can go on black runs and get down the slope with no fear, I know I can tackle it! There's a lesson in that. It felt like you were always there for me such as taking me to netball, listening to my struggles and difficulties, paying for school trips, and taking me away on many great holidays.

I remember you asking how I would feel if you took a job overseas. My response was to burst into tears, and I was so grateful that you chose to stay in England.

I was always very proud of your ability to fix things! You were a proper Dad. You could sort out the car, stuff around the house, repair our bikes, and your knowledge was passed on to both Iona and me. As a result, I have never been afraid to have a go.

I remember you cheering me on at netball matches and being very supportive of my sporting ventures. It always makes me smile now and laugh at your heckling in *all* the pantomimes you took Iona and I to.

I can recall the stress I would feel as I got older when driving with you! Your anger at other drivers . . . when often I'd be thinking this is not etiquette and that you were in the wrong!

And your eying up of the ladies! But also your ability to look beyond rules and regulations and make intelligent, safe decisions that would make life a little less mundane.

The day we heard Patrick (Churcher) had been murdered, we were (Meriden) and Mat his brother at the funeral, and knowing straight away they were related.

I remember you and Bernard crying with laughter over the same jokes and at Laurel and Hardy. Staying with you and Granddad and Bernard at 4 Exeter Road and often feeling very uncomfortable at meal times as there was usually competition between you two regarding who was going to hold forth. These dynamics completely changed as Granddad got older and you became respectful, and I remember thinking how incredibly kind and caring and competent you were when caring for your father in his later years.

There was always a part of me having to protect Iona from you and having strong memories of this as a teenager. These feelings are no longer felt because when you and Iona are together I see a healthy loving relationship, which gives me the proof that if you want to change aspects of your life, you can. You do not have to be a victim to your circumstances, especially once you arrive at adulthood. I think this trait of self-development that your father, you, and your ex-wife had has been passed onto your daughters.

I had a sense from quite young that you and Iona were far more similar and that Mum and I shared similar approaches to life.

Whenever I hear ABBA and Super Trooper I remember being in the car with you and Iona when we were driving to Aviemore to ski at New Year in 1980, when I was fourteen.

I think for my twenty-first, you took me to a restaurant, and the waitress brought out my birthday cake and all the customers sang happy birthday. Somewhere I still have the cork from the wine we drank that night.

I always feel regretful that I did not come to your wedding to Sue. I had some teenage social event to go to that was really irrelevant, but so important to me at that time but you live and you learn!

Memories of my Father—Iona Lyons

I remember being passed outside from my Mum to my Dad and being shown the garden completely under water (my Mum doesn't believe this as apparently it was the year I was born) I do though!

I remember age five and having a slight scepticism with the tooth fairy. I didn't tell either of my parents, and the next morning, there remained my tooth. I got up and told my dad, who was shaving in the bathroom. When I returned from the bathroom, the tooth had been replaced by a 5p piece: making me richer both financially and giving me an understanding of the ways of adults.

I remember my Dad coming home and giving a toy dog to my sister, when I asked where mine was, he didn't have one for me. The next day, when he got home from work, he presented me with a toy dog, but it wasn't identical to the one my sister had been given, so I cried as I wanted to be the same as her.

I remember running away from the bathroom when a strange man was there—turns out it was my Dad without his full beard.

I remember my Dad running down the stairs wearing a balaclava and really scaring me as I didn't know who it was and was unnerved by the speed he ran down the stairs. This started a big row between my parents, and I remember feeling miserable because I felt that it was my fault that they were rowing.

I remember my Dad telling my sister and I a joke about the surprise peas (what do you get with?) and chapped legs and watching him cry with laughter as we were more and more puzzled about the meaning of the joke.

I remember climbing out of bed and sitting at the top of the stairs with my sister holding her and crying, listening to my parents arguing downstairs.

At seven years old, I remember the day my Dad moved out and my Mum being outraged with the number of teaspoons he had taken. I remember I was very proud that I could direct my Mum to my Dad's new house in Gypsy Road after I'd been there only once. I had inherited my Dad's good sense of direction.

I remember going to my Dad's at the weekends and visiting the same stately home that we'd been to with my Mum the previous weekend. They had lots of secret places where monks could be hidden, which I already knew. To the delight of my Dad, I went round showing my Dad all the priest holes to the consternation and irritation of the guide as it was his party trick. I remember being devastated, on another of these weekends, when Dad snatched my favourite animal Ms Mouse from me and threw it into the river; fortunately, it was rescued, and it has now been passed to my daughter.

I remember the cutlery incident in our ski hotel when I dropped some knives and spoons in the dining room that Dad had asked me to take to our room—now every time I walk on a wooden floor I cringe. Maybe that's why I always forget the cutlery when I set the table—scarred for life! I remember the skiing holidays with Dad's friends—I didn't like Mike (Tucker) Dad's lodger because he didn't seem to like children, but I did like Pat (Churcher).

I remember Pat and Marie who lived over the road, and Pat became a very good friend of my Dad's and our family, until his untimely death in the late 1980s. I remember hearing about Pat's death when I was at my Dad's, when he came back from a run, throwing snowballs. Sue and I told him, and we all stood and held each other as it was such devastating news. I remember, as a result of that, Dad making plans for his funeral and his will and sending them to me and Kyla. It was a good example of how my Dad could make something positive out of a cruel and unjust situation.

I remember when Sooty, Dad's cat, died. He, Dad, showed me the gravestone he'd made as a memory to him. He was crying as he showed it to me, and I felt awful because at the time I had little compassion for my Dad and couldn't cuddle him or show him some affection when he needed it. When I was nineteen or so, I remember telling my Dad that we had lots in common, like jazz music and films and that we should ask each other about these things; to this day when I speak to my Dad, he often asks me what films I've been watching. This reflects his ability to take things on board. I remember watching my Dad watching Laurel and Hardy films and laughing at him laughing until tears rolled down his cheeks at the films. I found it really funny just watching him. I remember my Dad taking me and running with me on my cross country running races.

I remember arguing with my Dad when I was a teenager, and it felt like all the time and him saying 'ah you're exactly like your mother.' I look very much like my mother, but I think emotionally I'm much more like my Dad, which is probably why we argued so much. I can't remember what the arguments were about, but I remember when I said to him, 'I'm glad I'm like my mum because I'd hate to be like you,' he didn't say that to me again. I imagine that was hurtful to him, which, of course, as a teenager that's what I wanted to do as I was feeling hurt. Teenagers don't think of the consequences of their actions.

I remember talking to Sue, his wife at the time, about the arguments we would have, and she would listen and try and put his point of view across. Although the split between my Dad and Sue was such that I didn't want to keep in touch with her, although I feel very grateful to her for really helping my relationship with my Dad.

I remember watching fiddler on the roof and my Dad crying when a character died.

I remember writing my Dad a letter when I was in India because I found our relationship such a struggle; the letter took hours and many revisions with the help of my boyfriend, Bob. When I got home I asked Dad about it, and he asked me if I was drunk when I wrote it.

I remember when Marisa was one-year old, my dad had forgotten her birthday, so I told him off about this and saying that I wanted him to have a good relationship with his granddaughter as I had with his Dad, my grandfather. My Dad apologised and has never forgotten Marisa's birthday since.

I remember telling my Dad that I had left my husband because I was a lesbian. I remember him accepting my decision completely and feeling very supportive with his acceptance and understanding. After this, I remember my Dad asking me to go skiing with him and Kyla's family and saying no because I felt very uncomfortable. When he asked me why, he listened very carefully to my reasons and then apologised sincerely for his behaviour, although he had no memory of the incident.

I remember in the very recent past noticing the tenacity in which my Dad approached his convalescence following knee surgery and being very determined to make it better, constantly practicing his exercises and deep water running. I recognised those same qualities in myself that helped me recover from my chronic fatigue and helped me to build a fruitful and enjoyable relationship with my Dad.

I remembered things the other day when I was telling Emma what I'd written, and she asked whether you played with us much. I said oh yes, he'd take us swimming every week. We made the chess figures and you taught us both how to play chess and how to check the tyre pressure and oil levels in the car all very valuable!

It is said that you attract into your life what you need to heal in yourself, and I think that my relationship with my Dad has been a very good example of this.

Appendix 2

Marathon Reports, 1981-2011

Articles in Chronological Order

New York 1981; New York 2001 (seven weeks after 9/11); London 2002; London 2003; London 2004; New York 2004; London 2005; London 2006; London 2007; London 2008; London 2009; London 2010; London 2011; Keilder Water 2011.

New York Marathon, 1981

At last, my first New York City marathon in 3.48 wrapped in a big Union Jack with a chef's hat and beard (real) and two pairs of sox? This is the most iconic marathon created by Fred Lebow (Lebowski) 12 years earlier and deserving of special analysis. On the Saturday before I jogged the International Breakfast run, a tradition of NYC marathons where all the foreign runners, over 1,000 that year, assemble at the UN Building and accompanied by their respective flags, jog uptown on 5th Avenue to Central Park. That year we were treated to a magnificent buffet breakfast laden with every Manhattan breakfast items including donuts, bagels and lox, berry muffins, fruit salad, and so on. Even the tables were set out with a blow—up world as a centrepiece. If that wasn't all, we also given a commemorative 'T'-shirt and badge. Runners of all nationalities would meander around the tables exchanging pins and 'T' shirts from runs around the world. I exchanged some for two colourful South American ones. Then in the evening, we were all invited to a free Pasta Party in an enormous marquee in Central Park with great pasta bolognaise and beer and dessert. The atmosphere was just amazingly friendly with live entertainment and, of course, another 'T' exchange. Not however the best preparation for a marathon the next day!

New York really embraced the marathon across the city with warm up races weeks before and many restaurants and tourist attractions giving big discounts to the runners. Everywhere you went, New Yorkers would wish you well in the marathon—a marvellous feel-good climate to be in. You run through all five boroughs during the 26.2 miles starting off on Staten Island, then into Brooklyn over the Versarrano Narrows Bridge 1.5 k long with fire boats below shooting coloured streams as the runners pass overhead. A truly iconic and wonderful sight! After eight miles you enter Queens for about four miles and then over the forty-nineth St. Bridge into Manhattan (made famous by Simon & Garfunkel). Up 1st Avenue for a straight four miles stuffed with spectators and briefly into the Bronx. A lady with a placard announced 'run faster you're in the Bronx', the least inviting part of New York apparently! Then into Manhattan again down 4th Avenue into Central Park's undulating roads for the last four miles turning at fifty-fourth Street on the West Side to the finish at sixty-fifth Street near Columbus Avenue. Everything about the marathon was professionally organised by the New York Runners Club. Each year the Medals, 'T'-shirts, clothing, and general merchandise was specially designed by a well-known artist and was of a very high quality.

A Day to Remember and of Remembrance

The 32rd New York marathon, 4 November 2001

11 September was in sharp focus across Manhattan at 6.a.m. On Sunday 4 November, Dawn was some way off yet the US flags and bunting on cars, buildings, streets, and runners were a reminder of the patriotic fervour now in place for almost two months. On Saturday the 3 rd November, I had collected my number 1937 (my birthday year) & T-shirt from the security conscious marathon registration at the Jacob Javits Centre on W Forty-eighth Street. By some quirk, I had initially been given a wheelchair number and was given some disbelieving looks until the Trouble Desk took over. I then had my photo taken with the current marathon world record holder (two hours five minutes). Only two hours faster than me!

Next, Doug my NYC host biked me to Ground Zero where some 20,000 workers were still involved in the catastrophe aftermath—an incredible statistic. The devastated site apparently covers the size of twenty-seven football pitches! Numerous visitors to the site couldn't get too close but were reverentially quiet, and overawed. Many had poster maps to orientate themselves and understand which buildings had been destroyed—many more than just the Twin Towers. Help had arrived Statewide—I saw a cafeteria foodtruck from Baton Rouge Louisiana. Another local restaurant had closed its doors to commercial business indefinitely to feed the support workers, police, and firemen. Volunteer groups were also stationed twenty-four hours on the approaches to cheer the arriving and departing clearance trucks. All over Manhattan were places of remembrance where personal messages, photos, and tokens testified to the grieving of New Yorkers, US citizens, and Visitors.

The marathon starts at 10.40 a.m. from Staten Island's Fort Wadsworth where runners have to be in place by 8 a.m. the first arriving before 6 a.m. Sponsors provide hot and cold drinks, bagels, yogurts, and fruit for those not concerned with PBs (personal best times). Some 30,000 runners are provided with hundreds of portaloos; the longest urinal in the world (100 metres)—blokes only! Four-coloured coded start points and 50 UPS trucks for runners baggage taken to the finish. The temperature at 8 was around 50 °F and fine—very comfortable for most runners.

Security was exceptional with clear plastic bags for runners belongings. These were closely inspected—three times in my case and then my backpack was confiscated!

The route runs through all five boroughs of New York City—Staten Island—Brooklyn—Queens—The Bronx—finishing in Manhattan's Central Park at Seventieth Street. Mayor Guiliani had dashed back from the Yankees World Series defeat to give an impassioned and defiant send off after a Fireman vocalist sang the Star Bangled Banner and America the Brave—cheered loudly by the hyped up runners.

For the first two miles both levels of the Veranzano Narrows Bridge are used to cope—the wheelchair and female elites had started thirty minutes earlier.

The start gun fired, and I was only steps from the start line, so I settled into my eight minute mile (3.30) pace immediately—some back markers took ten minutes to cross the start. Down below in the New York harbour approaches, fire tenders were spraying red, white, and blue water forty feet high while up above a kaleidoscope of hot air balloons had the necks craning. Once into Brooklyn's 4th Avenue at about three miles, the runners crush thinned into two lanes with Peuto Ricans and Hassemite Jews in traditional dress, lining the route. Further on at seven miles and level with Liberty Island Police and Firemen crowded cherrypickers, exchanging cheers and waves with the runners while the crowds (estimated at around two million) waved Stars & Stripes (Old Glory) and handed out drinks, fruit, and sweets.

At eleven miles passing the Williamsburg Bridge, I'm slowing slightly to 8.5 minutes milling but still on a 3.45 target when a school steel band rocks into a calypso. The sun shines on the banners 'God Bless America,' and everyone is high on the occasion—even the out-of-condition runners.

We've now joined with the women and, with expected whoops and whistles, trudge over the Pulaski Bridge at thirteen miles and into the Borough of Queens in one hour fifty minutes, passing over the Long Island Expressway—known locally as the longest parking lot in America! I'm then passed by an 'old' lady at fourteen miles—has she really run over a half marathon? Transfers with 'I Love NYC Marathon' are stuck on runners' faces, legs, and arms. Through the short three miles of Queens then over the steep fifty-nineth Street Bridge (of the Simon & Garfunkel song), the only spectator-less part of the course. Then it's into Manhattan's 1st Avenue at sixteen miles. The noise is deafening with crowds lined six deep and with flags from around the world, cheering their runners—I move over to a Union Jack and get a roar of welcome. Briefly I speed up on the transferred adrenaline! It doesn't last, and I'm running on auto at eighteen miles up 1st Avenue—just a sea of runners straight ahead for four miles. More banners exhort 'no pain—no gain'. Briefly I run with another Brit from Watford and into the Bronx at twenty miles—'run faster' a women yells at me 'you're in the Bronx now'—a reference to the Bronx traditional high crime levels. My elapsed race time is two hours fifty minutes, and I'm still running within myself at nine minute milling—just! With 'only' 10 k to go, it's gritting teeth and digging in time but passing more and more walkers give some extra motivation to keep running—however slowly.

Now on the home stretch and back into Manhattans 5th Avenue over Madison Avenue Bridge and alongside Central Park at twenty-two miles! Then into the Park's undulating punishing roads with hordes of fans—some helping a distressed wheelchair athlete! At twenty-four miles another wheelchair participant, an elderly lady Brit, is tightly wrapped in a Union Jack and being pushed by two marathon volunteers. I give her a weak wave and greeting, and despite the crowds screaming encouragement,

I'm struggling to maintain a ten minute mile pace—but, rounding the bottom of Central Park at fifty-seventh Street, there's less than a mile to Shangri-la and the finish. It's now mind over matter—the legs are dead; the energy reserves have gone; and total exhaustion is not far away.

Then with 400 yards to go and passing the first-class grandstands, I spot Doug. He's in charge of the team of thirty Exit Guiders who 'escort' unnumbered runners off the course before the finish—and some don't go quietly! He gives me the thumbs up and then it's over the line in three hours fifty-five minutes forty-one seconds. It wasn't a great run (my fastest NY time is 3.10) but inside my target of shading four hours. After seventy marathons, I'm less exhilarated just pleased to do it and walk slowly again.

Then for no particular reason, I think of all those athletes who would have run but were trapped in the Twin Towers holocaust.

I'm handed the precious medal, wrapped in a space blanket, and provided a goody bag of eats and a bottle of water. Some runners are stuffing sandwiches—how can they? I keep walking to my UPS truck in case I cramp up and have a quick change before hailing a cab on Columbus Avenue at seventy-sixth Street. opposite John Lennon's memorial—Strawberry Fields.

Strolling New Yorkers acknowledge the medal around my neck—and maybe they've done it before and know how it feels.

My seventh and twenty-first anniversary of the NYC marathon! Will I do it again? Probably! But I'll decide after the pain and aches have subsided in a hot bath!

Some Race Statistics. Winners: Men—Testaye Jifar Ethiopia 2.07.43; Women—Margaret Okayo Kenya 2.24.21. Oldest finishers: Men—ninety-one; Women—seventy-eight.

Fastest in my age group sixty to sixty-four—Walter Koch Germany sixty-one. 2.47.44 phenomenal!

CODA Resulting from the 11 September, the finishers were down to around 24,000 (normally 28,000+)

London Marathon 14 April 2002—

A Lovely Day in the Sunshine

It's 8 a.m. on London's Blackheath cool but bright—just right for world records or in my case surviving with a little less pain. Jo and Verna have taxied me from Orpington my overnight stop as Dick, who normally shadows me around the 26.2, has very selfishly torn his Achilles on the badminton court. An elderly lady dog walker smiles across noticing my marathon gear, 'ah! I see the senior citizens are running'—cheeky beast!

We walk across to the Green Start, admiring the kaleidoscope of hot-air balloons, rising off the heath. My favourite is Bertie Bassetts liquorice allsorts—also my favourite confection. Of the three starts, red (Greenwich Park & funrunners), blue (Elites & 'youngsters') and green (ultravets & showbiz stars etc.), the green has only 2,000 runners, so even the backmarkers get over the start in two minutes.

Each runner sports a computer 'chip' attached to the shoe. This records time through the start, ten kilometres, fifteen miles, twenty miles, and, of course, the finish so taking short cuts is counter-productive and naughty. Also, waiting times at the start for the backmarkers aren't penalised as marathon times start as you pass over the computer mat.

In my case, as a mega sporting personality, I chat up a few soap and sports stars and sneak onto the front line—accompanied by Kip Keino the Kenyan superstar of yesteryear.

At the gun, I accelerate into my 100 yards dash mode and lead Kip and the field across 50 yards of grass—at which point, I get swallowed by a few hundred runners! Still I am nursing a backache sustained by gardening the previous Friday.

My target time is three hours forty-five minutes, so the first mile on Shooters Hill is passed at a leisurely 8.18 minute pace. The back is holding up well—my main concern.

We're now snaking through the streets of Charlton between two and three miles—damn those speed bumps but cheered by unusually large crowds. 'Ha Ha Road' (strange name) takes us along past the Woolwich Barracks before the drop into Woolwich where we're joined by the Blue start runners to choruses of boos and whistles nearing three miles. My pace has dropped slightly, so I go through the five in forty-two minutes but feeling good.

With about 35,000 runners, even the dual carriageway on the Woolwich Road is a bit cosy with too many trying to hug the blue (direct course) line.

I'm wearing cards with 'Dales 27th London Marathon' front and back and get many interesting responses from runners—like 'you must be mad', 'unbelievable', 'how come—This is only the 22nd!' 'fantastic' and 'how did you get in every year?'

The first rock band blasts out the decibels through Maze Hill with the crowd handing out orange segments/ice lollies and the ever-popular fruit chews. We then get the first Ogi! Ogi! Ogi! of the day as we circle under the Blackwall Tunnel flyover.

It's now about 55 f. with a hazy sun and very comfortable as the crowds build along Trafalgar Road into Greenwich and the Cutty Sark loop. In previous years, hundreds of marathoners were found taking shortcuts through the Greenwich Foot Tunnel to the Isle of Dogs to reduce the course by ten miles! Closer supervision of the Tube Stations en route and disqualification has nipped most cheaters—but 'why bother' is the question.

I'm joined by a Kiwi runner, and after I ask 'what part of Oz are you from?', he doesn't take too much offence. We run through the Isle of Dogs at ten miles in one hour twenty-six minutes and stay together until near the finish. En-route I find out he works in Canary Wharf, a walk from his 2 up 2 down terrace (currently priced at a staggering £250,000) at the eighteen-mile mark near Crossharbour on the driverless Docklands Light Rail. Halfway looms in the shape of the Tower Bridge packed four deep with screaming supporters 'go Trevor' '41034 Martin A1' 'Rachel—No walking!' and 'hello mum'. Dozens of charity supporters line this popular spot, waving flags, balloons, and placards. T.V. interviewers run alongside or drag out the Mickey Mouses, Rupert Bears (MD), and sports personalities who are feeling the pace and are glad for a breather.

As we pass the fourteen mile mark in 1.52 minutes, the fast frontrunners approach us across the carriageway—they've done twenty-two miles and are milling at about five minute pace! London's East End along the Commercial & West India Dock Roads is denuded of spectators and the point where many runners realise their training shortfalls—aching thighs, cramps, and still eleven miles to go! Through sixteen miles and into seething crowds enjoying the sun and beer and entertainment and glad they're not the ones suffering. An amazing modern sculpture of dozens of traffic lights flashing greets us into the concrete world of a rejuvenated Docklands and Canary Walk landscape. Here, the wind blows cold off the new marina docks, accelerated by the skyscraper towers—two more than last year. Runners are using the water stations for a breather; there are thousands of walkers through seventeen, eighteen, and nineteen mile-mark, and even at our 'leisurely' sub nine minute mile pace, we leave hundreds in our wake. It's a great feeling! The noise as we pass over the computer mat at twenty miles sounds like a room of chirruping budgies! I'm still on target in a time of 2.54 minutes—just under Westferry Circus and another chorus of Ogi! Ogi! Ogi!

Hey! Only six miles and a bit to go, and I'm not in pain—very unusual and means my training schedule has worked. Back through the East End and at 21 miles, we pass the fun runners across the road, struggling through the fourteen mile mark—poor sods! We exchange good luck cheers and waves. The ramp into Tower Wharf is the steepest part of the course—fortunately, it's only twenty yards but packed tight, over the cobblestones at the Tower of London and littered with cramped and exhausted runners. It's 'Show Time' for the St. John's Ambulance brigade. They do a great job massaging seized and aching muscles, and they're all unsung volunteers.

As usual the city is packed on streets, walkways, and bridges, watching and cheering the increasing number of walkers. Once under the Blackfriars tunnel, you feel you've cracked it as you emerge into the sunlight embankment. But where's my team, Jo & Sandra? They're nowhere to be seen at Cleopatras Needle so after a precious two minute search, I hobble off for the last mile: past Big Ben with the hands showing 1.12 and up Birdcage Walk with St. James Park packed with finishers. I'm struggling now, and the Kiwi left me at twenty-four miles so one last push—give the Queen a wave and then spurt 200 yards down the Mall to the finish—just outside my target in 3.53.22. *But* fifteen minutes better than 2001 and more importantly Hope and Homes for Children are over £700.00 better off—well done, Rugby Rotarians, family, friends, and villagers—another triumph!

Volunteers snip off the 'chip', on goes the medal, now now for a break! But no—to make matters worse, I'm accosted and interviewed by a BBC Scottish lady Heather Irvine 'Now tell me Dale how have you done twenty-seven London's when this is only the twenty-two?' *Good question!*

Dale (Galloping Gourmet) Lyons: race number 52,631; time three hours fifty-three minutes twenty-two seconds.

10,098th out of 32,889 (first 31 %); age group position 35th out of 221 (first 16 %)

Other facts: Winner male—world record. 2.05.37 K. Kannouchi, USA

Winner female and newcomer record 2.18.55 Paula Radcliffe GBR (only seconds outside the world record—impressive)

Oldest finisher male 92 years! Oldest finisher female 90 years!

23rd London Marathon 13 April 2003

The End of a Legend

The great event was overshadowed by the death of Chris Brasher, the London marathon founder. His wife was given the honour of starting the 40,000 record runners on a bright morning. It was rather too warm for running 26.2 miles from Blackheath to The Mall but not for the crowds gathered to watch the three starts—green for celebs, red for vets, virgins fun runners and foreigners, and blue for elites and everyone else. Paula (Radcliffe) our world record holder started at 9.05 with the elite women and decimated the field in a phenomenal 2.15, beating her own world record by an unbelievable two minutes; wheelchairs fizzed at 9.15 and the masses meandered out of Greenwich Park at 9.45.

My number was 30,008 in corral 4 and way back down Greenwich Way, but fortuitously I found myself ten seconds from the start after the gun went, along with another *everpresent* (those who've run every London). I'd done the training; viz. Long-distance races from twenty-six miles to a half marathon three weeks earlier, so I felt confident of beating my time of 3.53 in 2002. Ah how are the mighty fallen!

For the first eight miles just passed the Cutty Sark, and along the Creek Road in Plumstead, I was cruising at 8.4 minute miles and on target for a 3.45 marathon. Then inexplicably my times lengthened—the legs were heavier and ankles ached, and old gents, ladies, and portly youngsters passed me. By half way at 13.1 miles, my target had slipped to 9.5 minute miles and sinking rapidly. Was it the heat? Had I overtrained? Had I rested enough? Was my diet right? I couldn't figure, and the more I tried to improve, the worse it got. By the time I reached fifteen and through the Isle of Dogs into Canary Wharf, I felt ghastly with still eleven miles to go!

Survival time—drink plenty of water no improvement; try walking—even worse; have a rest—no I wouldn't start again!

Problem with going this slow after a 'decent' speed is the masses aren't very polite in passing—you collect lots of sharp elbows.

I was passed by Gorillas, Fairies, Spidermen, Wonderwomen, Father Christmases, and a weirdo with False Buttocks—how embarrassing!

Fortunately, I was past caring—by twenty-one miles, I was barely walking with 13.5 minutes milling, thinking only of the next step. Through the Tower Hotel over the Tower cobbles and into the City Road, I could hardly raise an *Ogi, Ogi, Ogi*, but neither could anyone else. I was absolutely knackered and in bits.

But rescue was at hand—at twenty-four mile (15.30 milling that's less than four miles per hour). Janet waved me down and supplied the 'Galloping Gourmet' chef's hat, pancake pan, and pancake. So after an alarming expletive which didn't faze the attendant Aussies, I shot off down the embankment tossing away and passed twenty-five miles around Big Ben to cheering crowds and up Birdcage Walk at something near eight minute milling—how was this possible? At twenty-four miles, I was fearing a five-hour marathon time. But, under the finish line, being almost brained by an enormous 'bottle of sherry' fun runner, and, tossing still, I finished in 4.49.39 seconds with a bare bummed Adam (fig leaf in place) just 'behind'.

Off with the (computer) chip on with the medal and a quick interview with Heather Irvine who reluctantly ate a piece of pancake, I was loaded down with a goody bag, containing twenty-three items, honest! I slowly changed standing up eating a boost bar, drank two litres of water and made my way slowly to the 'repatriation' area on Horseguards parade and a well-earned beer!

My 28th London (five more than anyone else)! My 66th marathon in my sixty-sixth year! It wasn't as spectacular as Paula's record but finishing again for the 23rd London felt just as good—oh Yes!

Dale's Time of four hours forty-nine minutes thirty-nine seconds was fifty-six minutes slower that last year. He came in 17,410th out of 35,000 finishers.

Who benefits?

Dale raised almost £650 for 'Bear Essential Aid' a charity that helps Ukrainian orphanages with toys, clothes, medication, medical supplies, and renovates water and toilet facilities with local labour in Ukraine. The present orphanage had 170 terminally sick, mentally and physically handicapped children who live only 40 km from Chernobyl the site of the worst nuclear power disaster in history.

2004 London Marathon—A 'World' Record Set

A new Marathon World Pancake Tossing Record was created in the 24th London (OAPs Section) on Sunday 18 April in a blistering time of four hours nineteen minutes fifty-seven seconds (unconfirmed) by Dale Lyons the Galloping Gourmet. It would have been faster but a waterlogged pancake slowed Dale down! Also you could have seen Dale on BBC Telly (twice) being interviewed by Ricky Pasad (12.30) and our Olympic Gold Medallist Sally Gunnell (hi-lites). Unfortunately, these interviews further slowed Dale's record time overall. He was, however, glad of the rest.

For the first twenty miles, Dale was cruising to a sub four hour finish with pancake flipping energetically—then a combination of mobile phone interference, the onset of drenching rain, pancake fatigue and general debilitation slowed him down through the Isle of Dogs and the City.

He was further disoriented by being passed by an assortment of second rate fun runners in the shape of Wombles, Telephone Kiosks, Geriatric ladies, Calender Girls, Superman, and worst of all Batman and Robin! However, he did not suffer the grosser indignity by being well ahead of IDS and Lord Archer—thank God!

Dale's time put him respectably in the first 50 % of finishers (15,883rd) with over 15,000 behind him! This was the 24 London marathon and Dale's 29 having run four doubles and one triple London on the same day—they're not all locked up yet! So it's now sixty-seven marathons and counting. To date, only twenty-nine runners remain who have completed all twenty-four London marathons since its inauguration in 1981 and are called the Everpresents (www.everpresent.org.uk) (see photo of some of them before the start).

At the finish, Dale was met by his partner Janet (speedy) Tomlinson and his daughter Kyla, Simon, and grand children, Joe and Anna, who were mightily impressed with the medal and soggy pancake—still edible. Afterwards, he had a fabulous welcome at the UK Cancer post-marathon reception and was treated to an elite massage and weak tea—fortunately just missing the torrential downpour which 'drowned' many late finishers (they should have run faster!).

The important thing is, over £420.00 has been raised for the Bobby Moore Cancer Fund, so Dale thanks all his generous sponsors—family, friends, neighbours, and fellow Rotarians. (Cheques should be made out to the 'Bobby Moore Fund—UK Cancer'.)

Dales next marathon will be in New York City in November—for the seventh time—but not tossing this time!

5 May 2004 Dale (Galloping Gourmet) Lyons

A Sunny, Runny, Funny Day in New York, 2004

Running number 17,862 set off for the New York City Marathon outside the 5th Avenue Public Library at 07.15 on a bus in a mild temperature of

53 °F on the 7 November 2004. Lengthy jams through New York and Brooklyn delay our arrival at Fort Wadsworth (the start) on Staten Island until 08.15. Security as you would expect is tight with only see-through plastic bags allowed for personal items. Numbers are closely inspected for all, but I still sneak in to the front line!

Today four sets of starts included mobile disabled at 9: wheelchair/handcycled—men and women, ladies, and lastly us at 10.15.

As runners arrive at six am by taxi, car, ferry (Battery Point), and bus, mountains of bagels and donuts, gallons of tea and coffee, and piles of yoghurts are freely handed out. I resisted them all! A centre stage provided assorted pop, rock, and blues (San Francisco Country Blues Band) to entertain and inform in the now balmy sunshine. Sectioned into red, blue, and green areas, the 37,000 odd runners were supplied with marquees, hundreds of portaloos, and the longest (200 yards) urinal in the world (for chaps only)!

I managed a great start, about fifteen yards from the start line after a throaty rendition of America the Beautiful across the enormous spans of the Verzaranno Narrows Bridge. Halfway across four NYC water tenders below spouted red, white, and blue plumes of water into New York Bay with runners risking serious injury stopping to take photos.

My first mile took 9.19 minutes and on target and speed up the second into Brooklyn (the second NY Borough) at 7.13 pace—too fast! From a gantry, a lady spectator yells 'you're all invited back to my place for pasta after'. The temperature has risen to 60 °F and warming up so on up 4th avenue thick with runners through the noisy Peurto Rican section while I settle down to a steady 8 milling up to the five mile mark in 41.33. Then just after five mile, the other half of runners join in (19,000), and the mass slows through the narrowing tortuous streets of Upper Brooklyn as we're stared at by Hassidic Jews in traditional long coats, tall hats, and hair in ringlets.

I'm still going well and get into Queens at the ten-mile mark in 1.25, although my pace has slipped to 9 milling—shades of things to come perhaps. We're all glad of the shaded streets as the sun is now hot, and we're nearing midday. We pass a hand-powered cycle, which looks very hard work, then it's over the Pulaski Bridge, past the halfway mark at thirteen miles, and into Queens, home of the New York Mets and Shea Stadium. I'm now feeling the effects of jet lag and lack of long training runs and slow to 10.30 minute milling with some large ladies passing me—curses!

The worst part of the marathon arrives in the shape of the fifty-ninth Street Bridge (famous for the Simon and Garfunkel song), which is over one mile long with a span that strangely rises for most of the length, has no spectators at all, funnels wind from the Hudson River, and is shaded by the top span so is quite chilly. I pass many walkers and exhort them to 'Go For It'. I get no response—what a surprise! Then into the sunlight and warmth and a veritable maelstrom of sound from the fifty-ninth Street bars and drunks! It's ear-splitting, and I've still got ten miles to go—Will I make it?

It's always a festival up 1st Avenue into Manhattan. And, for over four rising miles with fans standing five deep behind barriers, patrolled by New York's finest NYPD, my plod gets slower. The Dutch fans in their traditional yellow go berserk; others with placards saying 'Go Mum'—that won't apply to many, will it? The noise sanitises the increasing thigh pain as I slow again to a pedestrian at 14.24 minute pace at twenty miles in three hours eleven minutes. 'Gud Jaahb' (Good Job—NY speak) marathon volunteers scream—'looking good' others shout! Well, I don't feel it as we wheel around through the Bronx for a mile and into Manhattan's East Harlem and 5th Avenue. My upper thighs feel like blocks of wood as I stumble through the Gatorade water stations and take a relieving walk for fifty yards. I've now descended to a slow shuffle unlike Ali's Fast Shuffle and consider at this pace through Harlem I've another sixty minutes of agony. I lapse into a displacement strategy of relaxing in a hot bath and briefly have an out-of-body experience. Then immediately wonder why the next bloody mile marker hasn't arrived—I'm moving too slowly that's why!

It's long past enjoyment and into survival time, exhorting myself to move faster—swing those arms! Pick those legs up! Keep going! No walking! It works for a while, and I have a brief sigh of relief as I shuffle into Central Park at twenty-three miles, but it doesn't last. For those, like me who've done NY more than once—it's my seventh—Central Park is the sting in the tail. The three-mile route winds and undulates towards fifty-ninth Street and 8th Avenue but never seems to get there! You're dying and hate the massive crowds exhorting you to run 'you're nearly there,' they shout. 'I'm not, and it's not,' I reply, but it's a waste of precious breath—they can't hear me. I've now been running and lately much walking/shuffling for over four hours, and still there's two-plus miles to go. Each step is agony. Why do I do this to myself I wonder and can't think of any answer worth repeating—surely, it can't be that bit of metal at the end?

In the last mile, I've passed four comatose runners, oxygen masked on stretchers, and I thought I was in a bad way! With less than one mile to go along the bottom of Central Park, I'm keeping pace with the other walkers—the only thing is I'm running or trying to! A gigantic view screen materializes at fifty-ninth Central Park West showing runners in real time. I see myself waving on screen and start running faster. Suddenly, there's Janet my partner at twenty-six miles (she's been draughted in as a 'Bandit Catcher'—those who take out runners with no number), so I stop for a photo, a quick kiss, a cheer from the crowd, and dash at a frenetic nine minute mile pace to the line in 4.43.45. I don't feel much satisfaction, just relief. It's all over, and I look forward to that hot bath. Another marathon? Never again! What date's the London?

CODA. The very next day in the swish Tavern On The Green restaurant entertaining my NY friends, who should be seated on the next table? Yes, you've guessed—Paula and her family. Shortly after, Henrik Ramaala (the men's winner) joined her. Taking advantage of the heaven-sent opportunity, the attached photo of Paula, DRL and Henrik was the result. What a result!

Some interesting stats from the race.
My place overall. 19,463

Overall mile pace. 10.51 minute
Place in age group. 47th
Finishers. 36,544
Starters. 37,257
Finishers (%) 98 %
No. in age group 65-69 298
'80-89 8
Last finisher. 9.59.58 minutes
Winners Women's. Paula Radcliffe England 2.23.10
Men's. Henrik Ramalla South Africa 2.09.28

A Quarter Century of London Marathons 'The Great Bustard Flies Again,' 2005

Fortunately, the weather pundits got it wrong again. The 17 April 2005 dawned clear, sunny, and windless on Blackheath—perfect for the record 42,000 entrants assembled around the Churchill hot air dog.

The previous evening, fourteen of the twenty-nine Everpresents were feted by Dave Bedford, the Marathon supremo for supporting all 25 Londons with a lavish East End feast—plus a 'lecture' on how lucky we were to get automatic entry every year—thanks Dave!

This year, I spurned the Galloping Gourmet chef's gear and pancake in favour of the more flamboyant Great Bustard costume—my sponsored charity. In view of my five hour twelve minutes PW (personal worst) time, was this the right decision? Eggs from Russia are being hatched into Little Bustards (extinct in the UK for 200 years) and reintroduced to Salisbury Plains. So far so good eight years on for the Bustards!

Had I done the right training since my knee injections of hydrofluoric acid? A testing twenty mile Ashby race in three hours and long seventeen and twenty-two mile cross country runs were about right. So what went wrong? I was confident of a four hour time + or—ten minutes. My Bustard gear weighed a mere 1.5 lbs with little wind resistance. So was the problem a low carbo load?

The EPs (Everpresents) were given a green start, so I snuck into the celebs area, with ten minutes to go, and chatted to Master Chef Gordon Ramsey, who remembered me tossing (pancakes) in the Great North last year (after a little memory jog). The Cheeky Girls were just ahead—great motivation. And with a hard man from The Bill to one side, I was obviously in select company. The marathon attracts the great and the recognised with Sue Barker interviewing Steve Redgrave, and the EPs granted an official photoshoot under the green start line—thanks again, Dave.

The mayor of Greenwich officiated the start in some heraldic finery, which I had admired at close quarters earlier, and I was off flapping. Cruising through Charlton for 8.40 minutes first mile, I gradually subsided to ten minute miles by the 6th at Greenwich, and I already knew things weren't going according to the nine-minute mile plan. As I slowed, passing runners pushed and shoved past—inconsiderate b* * *s. Others, plus a few EPs gave a merry salute. Spectators pointed and laughed with 'Go you Bustard'—and other words! Children shouted—'look a duck!' I flapped onwards, increasingly disjointed. At ten miles, I passed a fallen runner. I learned later that a doctor acquaintance, who was also a 'virgin' marathoner, had given him the kiss of life. The fifty-nine-year-old was later pronounced dead.

Considering the numbers involved, that is, 572,000 finishers in twenty-five years, there have been few fatalities or serious injuries.

On to Tower Bridge at twelve miles, the legs feel they've done twenty-six. Then, Sally (Gunnell) for BBC TV stops me and asks, 'What's a Bustard?' I tell her, flap my wings, and stumble on. This year, the course has been 'improved' so no Tower, no cobbles, no Katherine Dock chicane, no Beefeaters, *plus* the whole of the city and docklands loop has been reversed—very confusing! Paula didn't like it either so take heed London!

I'd arranged to meet my daughters, Kyla and Iona, and grandchildren, Joe, Marisa, and Anna at Canary Wharf, the sixteen-mile mark, but as this was now the 18.5 mile mark, 'they'll have given up waiting,' I thought. Rounding the last bend before the Tower, there they were shouting and screaming, waving a decorative homemade Bustard banner and grinning a welcome—more I think from relief. I had a cooling draught of water and a chewy fig bar. Later I trotted off feeling fresher—grateful for the boost!

Eight miles to go seems forever especially as the miles had lengthened to fourteen minutes. My legs were leaden. But why? I asked. I'd done the training. No answer came there! Briefly, I was tempted by a notice 'free massage for those worn legs here'. Twenty of so male and female runners' legs were being caressed and soothed by oiled hands. A marathon official raised the tape when he saw me, but I stupidly resisted and stumbled on and into the last seven miles turning towards the city. Commercial Road stretches for ever through the East End's monotony—grime and lack-lustre parade of tatty shops and housing. However, we were briefly encouraged to see 'runners' passing on the other carriageway, eight miles *behind* us being chased by the marathon clean-up trucks—how embarrassing! By now the Bustard wings are chaffing my elbows, and I'm getting a sunburned neck after almost four hours—Jeez I should be finished and onto the beers already! Instead, I work out that I've another sixty minutes of suffering at least. I'm stopped again at 22.5 miles for another BBC interview and am glad of the brief respite. The next two miles are a blur enlivened by a roistering 'Ogi. ogi, ogi under Blackfriars tunnel. Along the embankment, the crowd is four deep and enjoying the shambling, walking, and stumbling (few are running) at twenty-four miles. Then there's my partner, Janet, her sons, Daniel and Pat, with Susannah and Jo, my friend, Dick, Ellen, and assorted supporters. As I cry out 'I'm b* * *cks', cameras flash, water is offered, well done is shouted, and I'm off for another 1.5 miles of agony. The legs have died so what's keeping them moving. Mind over matter, that's what! As Cleopatra's needle hoves into view, I suffer the final indignity—I'm passed by a taxi cab lookalike and worst of all the rhino—it's a very long time since the camel went by. The Bustard dies of shame!

At the finish, the Tannoy announces my arrival shortly followed by two Wombles. My time of five hours twelve minutes forty-six seconds. Is two hours fifteen minutes thirty-one seconds slower than my fastest marathon twenty-one years ago and my slowest single marathon of the sixty-one I've run to date? My seventieth will be a lot faster—you have my word!

I collect my bag off the last truck, of course, and am accosted by an Italian runner, who wants to know how many marathons I've done—despite speaking virtually no English. We converse in sign language writing numbers in the dirt. He has done sixty-five. Ha! I've done sixty-nine—molto bene! Feeling better I stagger off to find my family thinking—will I be back again next year! Of course, you will stupid!

Some race stats.

Women's winner—Paula Radcliffe 2.17.46 World record.
Men's winner (not English)—Fastest UK man John Brown 2.10. p.b.
Dales' split times—5 Mile forty-five minutes, 10 miles 1.37. Half 2.12, 15 mile 2.35, 20 mile 3.41. Last 1.2 mile 17 minutes! First half 2.12, second half three hours.
Average mile speed eleven minutes fifty-four seconds
'Everpresents' remaining, twenty-eight!

Dale (Galloping Gourmet) Lyons aka Great Bustard. As a result of some inspired sponsorship, the Great Bustard Group charity will be over £600 better off—well done, all my sponsors!

London Marathon 23rd April 2006—'No Wheels on My Zimmer,' but I Kept Rollin Along!

My thirty-first London Marathon (other Everpresents 26) was completed in the relatively slow time of 4.45.04 on a rainy but mild day. However, I was carrying (yes carrying) a standard Zimmer frame as my wheeled version was judged ineligible by London Marathon Ltd. I did attempt to get special dispensation for the zimmer and aged concern but to no avail. 'You'll be disqualified and banned for life' was the kindly reminder of the rules!

So it was a case of 'No wheels on my wagon' for 26.2. As a result, I rigged up a harness from found bits the night before and up kept a steady 10+ minute milling all the way due to my rigorous training, general superb fitness, and a handy store of jelly babies! After twenty miles, they perform miracles—honest!

Before the start, the Everpresents met at the Greenwich Park Grandstand for a group photo—but, unfortunately, only ten showed.

During the run, the spectators and runners gave me fantastic support, and many couldn't believe I was carrying a zimmer. 'Vos ist das?' A German runner asked—'ja woll' I responded. 'Les Anglais sont fou!' two French runners commented. 'Qui, mais je n'est pas le trop fou,' I replied, thinking of St. George pulling the Dragon, who is going to take a week to finish! They're not all locked up yet, are they?

Not having had time to practise on the wheel-less zimmer, I'd little idea of the possible problems en route, so I kept to a relatively sedate pace early on. The neck strap I'd attached slipped around a bit until the rain fixed it, and at fourteen miles, I stopped and raised the height to stop it grounding. After that, it was mind over matter.

Again, the route had been changed again this year just to confuse the masses, so at 12.5 miles, the route took the right hand of Commercial Road into the East End and into the Isle of Dogs loop the opposite way, exiting past Canary Wharf, which as usual was jammed to the rafters. The noise was deafening!

Then under the Blackwall tunnel underpass and later the Blackfriars underpass, I managed to kickstart an *ogi, ogi, ogi,* the runners marathon chant. In fact, it's become so popular a DJ en route near the eleven-mile mark exhorted passing runners to *ogi,* and naturally they responded.

The London has now become as much a street party as a marathon run. Along the route, spectators had dressed up and waved flags, placards, names 'Hello Dad', and the burgeoning charity worker groups with masses of message balloons, screaming their heads off when their runners passed. Big bands, brass bands, steel bands, disco music, bagpiper groups, rock groups, and R & B bands—you name it they were there with the spectators urging the runners to go faster than their fading legs would carry them.

Helpful runners offered and passed me drinks—taking pity on me with some running and chatting with me for a while. Distractions like that helped to pass the time and displace the pain!

Surprisingly, despite my partner, Janet, and friends, Dick and Ellen, being at the Cutty Sark (7 miles), Island Gardens on the Isle of Dogs (16 miles), and near Cleopatras Needle (25 miles), I never saw them, even though they saw me. Unless spectators have some clearly noticeable marker—big notice, large balloons, giant umbrella, and so on—runners just see a sea of faces flashing past. Despite the rain, the course seemed more crowded this year with hardly a gap on the twenty-six miles. For first-time runners or those whose training hasn't been enough, there's plenty of carbo nourishment on the route—apart from the official lucozade stands—such as orange segs., bananas, chewits, lollypops, mars bars, and best of all jelly babies, which give you a real sugar surge—especially for those who *really* hit the wall!

I'm now known as the zimmerman—what a burden—and was very briefly interviewed on BBC TV, by Colin Jackson (ex-world record holder) on Tower Bridge at the twelve-mile mark. He was rightly gobsmacked by my attire and almost lost for words.

I was still running around ten minute milling from twenty, so I had the really delightful feeling of passing hundreds of static, walking, shuffling runners—not so nice when you're one of them! The miles at this 'speed' seem to flash by. I stopped briefly at the aged concern groupies at twenty-five-mile mark who collectively gave me a rousing cheer and thumbs up—I speeded up, briefly!

At the finish, the crowd raised a cheer as the route DJ called out 'here's the Zimmerman', and crossing the line, Sally Gunnell shouted 'well done, Zimmerman'. Off came the computer chip (no chip no time) which gives your personal times from the start and at 10 km, 25 km, 35 km, and the finish—this removes the previous anomaly whereby delays for the backmarkers were added to your overall time.

Finally, the London Evening Standard met me for a follow-up to their Friday article on the Everpresents. Got the medal over the Galloping Gourmet hat and felt really good! The Zimmer felt better!

At the aged concern HQ, they were over the moon with the TV publicity and provided lots of TLC with lovely cups of tea, buffet snacks, massage, photos, and seats!

> Anyway, most importantly, I've raised over £800 so far for aged concern—I might need them sooner than later, so I'd like to thank all my sponsors unreservedly for their generosity, good wishes, and support before, during and after the marathon. Well done!
>
> Many thanks and best wishes.
>
> Dale (Galloping Gourmet) aka Zimmerman

Overall this was my 71st marathon, and it seems the Everpresents are now down to twenty-four as four either didn't start or finish. So bring on 2007!

26 April 2006

Dale's run statistics. 10 miles one hour forty-five minutes, 13.1 miles two hour thirteen minutes, 20 miles three hour thirty-one minutes.

Last 6 miles one hour fourteen minutes. Overall mile pace, 10.87 minutes. Finish time 4:45:04.

Marathon Report 2007—The Hottest London Ever!

'Some Don't Like It Hot!'

Warning! 'Marathon running can damage your health'. Forecasts for the 2007 London Marathon were for high temperatures, so start well-hydrated and drink regularly en route was the advice. Over 5,000 runners were treated by medics: seventy-three were hospitalised, three were in critical condition, and one has since died, aged twenty-two after finishing the race.

This was the hottest London ever with temperatures off the ground reaching 23.5 °C. One week previously the Rotterdam Marathon had been terminated after 3.5 hours due to temperatures in excess of 28 °C so the warnings were there.

This year I decided to do something unusual for me. That is, give my generous sponsors a year off and run a no-frills marathon just for 'pleasure' and enjoy the race. No pancake, no zimmer, no bustard, no egg, spoon, and so on. How wrong my expectations were to be on the day!

For fourteen miles, all was going to plan. I'd met twelve other Everpresents (fellow nutters who've run every London) in Greenwich Park (red start) at 8.30 took photos and had a swift start—over the line in five seconds. I'd planned nine minute mile even pace running expecting a finish of around four hours. Well, I'd finished the 1st Draycote Marathon two months earlier in four hours thirteen minutes with little long-distance training, so why not?

The first five miles drifted by in forty-six minutes punctuated by the local priest, sprinkling us with Holy Water and tots looking for high fives. Crowds were the biggest ever I've seen and with brass bands, jazz bands, steel bands, rock bands, drumming bands every couple of miles—the noise was deafening. At ten miles, I'm still enjoying the run and go through in ninety-four minutes just off the nine minutes pace. Then at Tower Bridge, I even have time to chat with BBC TV's Colin Jackson, telling him I've run more London's than anyone—I don't think he believed me because it wasn't broadcast—c'est la vie!.

I'm drinking much more than normal but don't feel particularly hot or uncomfortable. In fact, I pass a couple of EPs (Everpresents) around ten miles after a chat. 'Gebrselassie has just retired at nineteen miles,' said one listening on his walkman.

Cold shower tents to run through had been placed on the route starting at nine miles, which most runners took advantage of. Vittel water stations at every two miles interspersed with Lucozade stands had been added to combat the heat and were a blessing.

But what happened at fourteen miles? I just got slower—twelve minutes milling and slower, fourteen minutes at sixteen miles, fifteen minutes at eighteen miles, sixteen minutes at twenty miles, peaked at 17.5 at 21—that's not even a decent walk pace, and I'm trying to run! I try a 'faster' walk for two miles and 'speed up' to fifteen minutes pace. By which time, I've been passed by Fred Flinstone carrying his buggy, assorted fairies, assorted clowns, a bedraggled Elvis, a lively Santa Claus, a Pantomine horse. 'B* * *ks,' I thought, I'm passed caring as long as I finish! I've now got a pocketful of jelly babies and juicy fruits to keep me going from thoughtful spectators—bless 'em.

Some others aren't so lucky. All around from twenty-two miles, stricken and exhausted runners are being given emergency treatment—some look in a serious state. St. John's Ambulance volunteers are fully stretched with runners' queuing for treatment—I'm tempted to stop but resist. At twenty-three miles even at my pedestrian pace, I'm passing dozens of runners some on their last legs. Many runners are being physically helped along by other runners, but I wonder—shouldn't they be getting treatment instead!

Now at twenty-four miles, I must be hallucinating the mile markers seem to be arriving quicker. I even manage to raise an *ogi ogi ogi* in the Blackfriars underpass and get a magnificent response—probably because there's only two miles go.

Crowd of three and four deep still line the course and are more vocal—encouraging the crawling runners to keep going. 'You're nearly there,' they cry! 'Come on Bob, Carol, Dave, Barry, Mum, Dale'—oh that's me! Two miles might just as well be ten to some about to reach total exhaustion. I saw one young lady being wheeled away by St. John's with only a mile to go—agonising!

Dale, Dale, Dale, I hear as I stumble through Parliament Square. I turn back to see Janet, my partner, and Dick, all smiles and relief. They expected me about ninety minutes ago. I stop briefly for a drink, a 'well done', and a kiss (from Janet) and charge off up Birdcage Walk, rejuvenated with aching limbs forgotten. Past the Palace—where's a wave from QE2? Down the Mall and through the finish in five hours twenty-five minutes thirty-eight seconds, my slowest single marathon ever! I'm blaming the heat and something I'd rather have left in Lagos!

Now—what shall I do in 2008?

Dale's race stats. First 5 miles forty-six minutes, second 5 48 minutes, third 5 52 minutes, fourth 5 77 minutes, fifth 5 82 minutes.

First half. two hours four minutes, second half three hours twenty-one minutes

Londons completed 32 (27+5)
Marathons completed 73
Position overall 20,958 59 %
Position in age group O/70 67th
Total finishers 35,674 Highest ever!
Men's winner Martin Lel Kenya. 2.07.41
Women's winner Chun Zhou China. 2.20.38
Bottles of water supplied 750,000

Flora London Marathon 2008
'A Crutch for the Waterlogged Gourmet'

Or 'Have Pancake Will Jog'

After twenty-seven (or thirty-two if you count the five extras), London's you'd think I'd be a rather complacent marathoner; absolutely not! Why? My knee op. that went wrong meant few long training runs and a regularly aching knee hence the crutch and knee support. I know I could have abandoned the 'tossing' but getting a laugh eases the pain. Anyway, I had ample supplies of ibuprofen on board if needed.

I had practised with the crutch and tossing round the local streets and what strange looks you get in Harborne—you'd think they never seen a jogger before!

Anyway back to the FLM, the green (celebs) start. 2,000 runners and very cozy! Photo with the Masai warriors whose assegais were a bit sharp! Their footwear looked like Mini tyres and probably were! A bottle of beer shook my hand (it was an idiot inside a Fuller's pale ale costume); a basketball dribbler first timer was mightily impressed I'd completed twenty-seven: as was a trio of Flora employees from Mexico who weren't impressed that I didn't eat large quantities of Flora produce daily.

Nine Everpresents showed up for a group photo in our personalised sponsored 'T'-shirts, now down to twenty-three owing to one more dropout.

After taking two minutes to the start line, I eased into the crutch or toss pattern until upended in front of the first mile marker. Narrowly getting trampled by 10,000 runners, I retrieved crutch, pan, and pancake, shrugged off the immediate trauma, and concentrated getting through the next 25.2 miles without further delays. At three miles, all three start streams merge to good natured booing and catcalling with the first *ogi, ogi, ogi*'s resounding around the Woolwich streets. Despite trying to settle into twelve-minute milling, the first five in warm sunshine flashed by in under fifty-four minutes because the crowd surge pulls you along faster than you want to go.

With water stations every mile, there's always a danger of over-hydrating—witness the fatality in 2007 even with 250 ml bottles. My intake was about 120 ml every—three to four miles as a top up.

Where was Janet at six miles? She was there but missed me in the river of humanity nearing Greenwich and the Cutty Sark, which was shrouded in tarpaulin and scaffolding. Oops—then we all come to a grinding halt on the loop and inch slowly into Creek Road where the charity groups go mental at my double and triple flips!

At eight miles, a cloudburst soaks everyone, including the pancake so tossing was suspended for an hour. I was relieved to have my heli-hansen thermal and gloves—whereas some 'naked' runners must have been almost hypothermic in the really chilly wind and driving rain. Onto the Tower bridge at twelve miles, the rain relented, but I was on the wrong side for the BBC camera crew—*drats*! Looking down for the potholes ensnaring my crutch, I noticed an aborted computer chip. 'No chip, no time' for that runner. The FLM must come up with a better system for chip retention (on the shoe). e.g. the Ashby twenty, I ran recently had the chip integrated into the running number—Dave Bedford, please note.

Through halfway at 13.1 miles and the tossing resumes to the heightened amusement of the roaring crowds, crushed mars bars, orange segments, jelly babies, water bottles, and gloves litter the route. Increasingly, I'm congratulated by passing runners as an Everpresent, mostly by attractive young ladies but also by another geriatric who had done fourteen Londons but insists on taking a photo before shooting off like a spring rabbit.

Last year, mile 15 on the Isle of Dogs started my dramatic decline. This time at the sixteenth, I called Janet, my partner, that I was on schedule and then speeded up. The sun was out again, the pancake full of life, and the crowd full of beer and encouragement—I felt great and ready for the next four to the twenty mile watershed.

This is the marathon 'Death Zone', that is, *the wall*. St. John's volunteers are really stretched with treating cramps, blisters, fatigue, nausea, muscle failure, and much worse—on seeing a prone runner lying where he fell surrounded by medics and St. John's. Not enough training? Too much? Too fast? Who knows?

At nineteen miles, the BBC TV interviewer wanted to know why the crutch, pancake, and Everpresent vest. I've lost my voice but manage a garbled 'running for Acorns Children's Hospice in Birmingham' and totter off cursing.

It's good getting past twenty miles and overtaking slower runners—great feeling!

Now the countdown! But with almost four hours gone down again comes the freezing rain. My visibility is almost nil—can't see my Timex so stop at twenty-one miles under the rail bridge and call Janet whilst asking an obliging lady spectator to nurse the pan. Then through the rain into the city at twenty-three miles and in the centre of a mass of runners—with again a waterlogged pancake! Where's the respite of the Blackfriars underpass? Dodging the puddles and grabbing another Lucosade energy drink 'I make it through the rain and kept myself protected' in the underpass. I try an *ogi, ogi, ogi*, but not a sausage of a response. I try again but no luck; they're all totally knackered.

Into the sunshine, what joy at twenty-four miles up the 'hill' and onto the embankment but no Janet. She did see me but with viewers four deep, she got crowded out again.

I'm passing hundreds who can hardly raise a walk while I sail along at 5.5 mph crutching and tossing knowing I've about fifteen minutes to finish. Then past Cleo's Needle under the Embankment Bridge and through twenty-five miles, threading through the deafening masses en route. It's unbelievable really—you should try it!

In a flash, it's Big Ben, Parliament Square, Birdcage Walk along Green Park, and past the Palace. But where's HRH Elizabeth? She'd get a great view from the balcony.

Twenty yards to go, and I drop the pancake to spectator oohs and aahs. On aching thighs, I scoop it up and flip through the Finish in 5.18.17.

Well done! Terrific! Keep tossing! Good jab (USA)! Magic! Volunteer responses as I'm relieved of my timing chip and given my 100th Anniversary medal. Can I have another one for the crutch? 'You having a larf,' the volunteer smiles. I stagger on and collect the goody bag and baggage. Really the five plus hours are over in a flash, and the knee surprisingly wasn't a problem. The spare pancake remained untossed!

Unfortunately, the Everpresents are now down to 22—2 more dropouts this year.

So will I be back for another London in 2009? What do *you* think?

Dale's stats

Overall time 5:18:17. Bang on schedule!
First 13.1 2.32.05, second 13.1 2.46.12
Overall position. 20,967 position in age group o/70 65th.
'Speed' first half 11.7 minutes per mile, second half 12.7 m. p.m. Overall 12.15 m. p.m
Conclusions
Around 11,000 runners *behind* me including the Masai Warriors and Adam + Snake.
No blisters. Eight minutes faster than last year.
Male winner Martin Lel 2.05.15 only 3.12 minutes ahead of me!
Female winner Irina Mikitenko 2.24.14
Sponsorship for the Acorn Children's Hospice raised £800 from friends and family. Rugby & Edgbaston Convention Rotarians & Inner Wheel ladies and Clocktower French Class & Fircones French Class, well done you all—I'll be back next year for another good cause—you bet!

29 London Marathon, Sunday 26 April 2009
'Crutches to The Fore—A Run On Four Legs'

What a glorious day it turned out after the diabolical weather predictions. Hot-air balloons on the Heath and portaloos by the thousands—what more could you want?

With little training, owing to clapped out knee and underarm crutches that were abandoned at enormous expense, I turned to DWR (deep water running) loadsa gym work and a modicum of crutch practice to keep my Everpresent status intact with twenty-two remaining at kick off.

Dick dropped me off near Blackheath Village, a short walk from the Heath. But the start area (three start points red, blue, and green) is now so restricted and convoluted I had another fifteen minutes crutch to my green start area. Ah! for the halcyon days of 1981 when you could park 30 seconds, from the Greenwich Park start and only 4,999 runners (no women). Still, that's the price of success!

Only twelve of the Everpresents showed for a photo—all complaining of restricted training, but with my crutches, I had the edge. This start is supposed to be for celebs plus a few geriatrics &and virgins (first timers), so it's a comfortable 2,000 field.

Gordon (Ramsey) gave me a dismissive look of recognition. The other crutched athlete, an wounded officer from Afgan service said he would take 2 weeks to complete at two miles a day—amazing! A Flora Marathon rep., Ben, with whom I'd been involved, introduced himself. A group of twenty-four linked Welsh runners said they were attempting a Guinness record—nuff said. Blind Dave Healy walked straight past me until I cried, 'Blind Dave!'—then we chatted. Finally, I allowed the Mayor of Lewisham who was starting our marathon to be photographed with me.

It was a leisurely start with me crutching at the rear but still passing someone who was walking after halfmile! Then chaos as the blue start runners joined in at the one-mile mark. Similarly, just as the pace had settled, we got to Woolwich, and in came the red runners to catcalls and boos.

I was hopping, lopping, and crutching along at a steady 4½ mph pace checking on the many pothole hazards. My knee felt comfortable, although my right hand was losing feeling.

Janet, my partner, was supposed to buzz on the hour—nothing, so at seven miles, I tried her mobile to learn they had arrived at the six mile! Hey ho—the best laid plans and all that. I'm getting phenomenal support from the passing runners and spectators due to my Everpresent status and crutches—very encouraging. Coins, missing charity buckets, discarded bum bags, wigs! T-shirts littered the route. As the heat built with no shade or breeze I loped towards Greenwich and the moth-balled Cutty Sark at seven miles.

I slowed to 4 mph stopping at every other water station and got passed by six joined up runners in a Hearing Dog costume—God, I thought, 'they must be baking'. Then my first (lady) Rhino past—I could tell from the hairless thin legs and running style.

Displacement is a always a good way to minimise pain, so for the next three miles, I fantasised about the delicious meal we'd booked in the tapas restaurant.

Just before Tower Bridge, I stopped for my second round of painkillers and was then interviewed on the Bridge by a gobsmacked BBC TV personality Rob on seeing a crutched 'runner'.

At 12 ½ miles, the route is a dual carriageway for three miles with the fast guys and gals fizzing past having already completed twenty-two miles—showoffs! At the halfway mark, I've been crutching for 3 hours 4 minutes, so my ETA should be around 6 ½ hours and well under the cut-off time. My team is no shows again at fourteen miles, which is very distressing when you're expecting some TLC. Anyway, they eventually appear at fifteen, West Ferry—Isle of Dogs *and* with no jelly babies. Then we're into the docklands four mile loop which drags on interminably. I've slowed to around fifteen minutes milling, that is, 4 mph but feeling OK. One problem with crutches, you can't grab assorted offerings from the spectators such as jelly babies, orange segments, juicy fruits, cans of lager, ice lollies, and so on, most of which are not really advisable 'treats' during a marathon.

The noise around the Canary Wharf is deafening echoing off the skyscrapers with watchers screaming out Da-el; Da-el; Da-el; as I limp past, I'm getting the sympathy vote for the crutches! Slow as I am I'm now passing assorted walkers and others collapsed on the pavement, some throwing up, most exhausted others being aided by the redoubtable St. John's—they're a godsend! Through Canary Wharf, I then leave Peter Andre and Jordan surrounded by media and minders, in my wake.

Only eight to go as someone trips over my crutch, I stop to pick it up and a blind runner's partner offers his water bottle—how nice! My team Janet, Dick, and Ellen eventually show up at twenty-one miles to take some photos and dole out water and TLC but again no jelly babies.

'You're amazing, incredible, fantastic, unbelievable, well done, good job, runners call out as they read the T-shirt 29 Londons and ran every one—Everpresent.org.net.' Well, as Max Bialystock said in Mel Brooks filmThe Producers 'if you've got it—flaunt it!'

The runners have thinned significantly through the East End and along Commercial Road, but the crowd won't leave as they cheer another Elvis ah—hu—hu ing all the way. I get on the shoulder of Barak Obama at twenty-three miles, but he pulls away embarrassed to be overtaken by an invalid. On the adjacent carriageway other walkers and fun runners are still ten miles behind the crutches—when will they finish? At dusk probably!

Then, just as I'm making a push for the tape—excruciating cramp in my right thigh and another in my right calf, I stop to ease and massage the pain away, taking off the knee strapping. I'm now hobbling at less than 3 mph. Where's St. John when you need him? He or she turns up at 23 ½ miles approaching Blackfriars so I succumb to the soothing hands of a matronly lady for five minutes—any longer and I might not leave.

With a last gasp through the Blackfriars underpass, I give out a cri de coeur *ogi, ogi, ogi*, to which a few stragglers gamely respond and into the sunshine of the embankment with two miles to go.

All along and under Waterloo and Hungerford Bridges, the charity groupies and a faster EP give me a fantastic lift, then its past the Sri Lankan protesters in Parliament Square, up Birdcage Walk passed Buck. House (no wave from HRH), past a sign saying *only 385 yards to go* and down the Mall to the glorious finish line with hundreds behind me. Just before the line, I stop and give a crutch bow to the phalanx of camermen. It doesn't seem like 29 years since I completed the 1st London—where did it all go?

That's it! Next year I'm taking it easy in a wheelchair as it's downhill all the way! Or am I? Whatever—roll on 2010—and the redoubtable twenty-one Everpresents.

Congrats to Pat Dobbs first O/70 o/o 94 3 hours 31 minutes 03 seconds. Phenomenal!

Later I learned the Everpresents have lost another so we're now down to twenty-one. Check all the marathon info, photos, stats, runners on our website www.everpresent.org.uk

Dale's stats. Official finish time. 6 hours 40 minutes 53 seconds.

First half 3.04.32, second half 3.36.21
Average speed. 15.30 minutes 3.92 mph.
Fastest mile. 12.42 minutes 4.70 mph
Overall position 34,546th position in age group +70 cat. 84th o/o 94.
Finishers. Total 35,247, men 24,230, women 11,017
Slowest logged finisher 8 hours 50 minutes 41 seconds. Dan Tarawik (GBR)
Number of unlogged finishers unknown.
Logged runners in Dale's wake 701, men 292, women 409

London Marathon Report 2010, the knee rules OK!

The forecast was for blue skies and temperature around 22 °C, so naturally it was cool and raining heavily before the start! At 8.30 fourteen Everpresents were interviewed on BBC TV with Jonathon Edwards who asked 'you're not tossing that thing, are you?' referring to my pancake. 'No', I said 'it's just for the interview'. The Mayor of Greenwich set up off at 9.45, and after a leisurely start at the back, I briefly chatted with Richard Branson (dressed as a butterfly), leading Princess Beatrice's 'caterpillar' going for a Guinness record for the fastest group tied together. Along with these exhibitionists was the 15' high Angel of the North and a lookalike giraffe going for the tallest entry at about 20'. As my new bionic titanium knee was 45 weeks old and an unknown quantity for the distance, I decided to race walk and set off at a 12.5 minute mile pace with my Everpresent colleague Dave Fereday, a veteran of this technique.

The starting arrangements for this marathon, for those not in the know, there are three starts for the 37,000 field. Red numbers go from Greenwich Park (22,000) including fun-runners; blue from Blackheath (14,000) including male and female elites, and wheelchairs and green (2,000) personalities, VIPs, and geriatrics, for example, Everpresents. The starting line-up is wheelchairs first, ladies, and then elites and everyone else at 9.45.

After one mile, the greens merge with blues at Shooters Hill when chaos reigns. Route marshals man the road humps, and things settle down for another two miles when the reds converge just above Woolwich. Each group jeering and whistling good naturedly at the other! Shortly before this, I'd 'speeded' up to 11.40 minutes mile pace and lost Dave, never to see him again! In the event, he passed me at about the seven or eight mile marker. I'm enjoying the atmosphere. The weather has improved, and the crowd is in great voice 'get a move on' one shouts. At this stage, the runners are about thirty abreast and most are passing me at a lick doing 9/10 min. miling to my 12. Oops, someone has dropped their mobile, I just avoided stepping on. I doubt it'll be in good shape for long. One thing puzzles me at two miles. There is an enormous queue of runners at a bank of portaloos. Why didn't they go before the start?

My training this year until 3 months before was on target until sciatica and ham strings injuries laid me up. I could hardly walk, so I tried Chinese massage, sports masseurs, osteopathy, and low-frequency pulse treatment. All of this got me back to training only five weeks before the big day which gave no time for the long (twenty mile) runs I needed. My max was fifteen with speed infills, so I knew that at sixteen in the marathon, I would have to wing it. With 29 Londons in the bag, my experience, I reasoned, would pull me through. Also my team would cheer me en route (Janet, Dick, Ellen, and in the later stages my daughter, Kyla). Advanced technology was also on hand in the shape of my other daughter, Iona, who could track my progress on her i-phone through the computer mats every 5k. These mats link to the runners' computer shoe chip and provide an exact timing for every runner. Cool, n'est pas?

There are also a number of blind runners with guides every year, and around the five mile mark, I passed one. A few seconds later, the same pair barged into my back, and I had to resist saying, 'can't you look where you're going?' Although I didn't see them, some runners were carrying fridges, ladders, and a tiger (stuffed replica). As if just running, 26.2 miles wasn't enough. At the twelve mile mark on Tower Bridge, two runners are dragging a sledge with a wall on it with a 'break-through' company message on it. 'Whatever next,' I asked myself narrowly being run over! Turning into the Commercial Road at twelve miles, the fast guys are running through twenty-one in the other lane, and I thought they'll take about 3.5 hours; I went faster than that in the eighties!

Anyway I'm through the half in 2 hours 53 minutes and slowing up with my miling around 14 minutes but feeling good and still in control. My supporters give me a lift at fifteen mile but have no drinks or take no photos—what am I paying them for? I give a timely *ogi, ogi, ogi* at the Commercial Road underpass and get a soto voce response. The drink stations are running low as the temperature rises. I'm starting to overtake loadsa walkers, which feels good. I take a handful of jelly babies from a large lady and take my second hi carb jell, which provides a much needed boost through to twenty. I'm jogging at fourteen minutes milling, feeling good with the bionic knee in good shape too. An ambulance screeches through, and I see a runner vomiting curled up and in bad shape surrounded by St. John's aids. Large queues of runners line up for the portaloos this side of Canary Wharf, and I think 'if they wait too long, they'll seize up.'

So far we've past jazz groups, big jazz bands, steel bands, very noisy drum bands, brass bands, salsa bands, pop groups, boy cadet bands, yes they're all out there playing to the biggest audience they will ever play to. And, new this year a gyrating or swinging scantily clad group of young ladies——head turners all.

Spectator banners vie for notice—taller, wider, more colourful, now with photos, exhorting their runners 'well done, son!' We're now over five hours into the marathon around Canary Wharf and houses, streets, and buildings are still crammed with spectators shouting themselves hoarse. I'm jogging along at a leisurely fourteen minutes milling and passing '00's of runners many the worse for wear and still six miles to go. The clear up trucks are out; the millions of discarded bottles are being emptied by the volunteers and bagged up. Steam hosiers are vainly trying to remove super-glued gel packets from the road.

Passing the Tower of London a lonely beefeater shares some sympathy with an exhausted walker. The City of London streets and along the Embankment are still packed, and suddenly, I hear 'Daddy' screamed from the pavement. It's my daughter, Kyla, who finally made the route at the twenty-five mile mark so we exchange hugs and arrange an Admiralty Arch meeting.

Up Birdcage Walk and passed the Q. V. monument, Buckingham Palace and down the Mall. But where's H. R. H Elizabeth 2? This is the thirtieth time she's failed to give me a wave—honestly! No-one looks up from the press box as I signal thirty completed. They're all waiting for the Gingerbread Man whom I'm well ahead of at 26.2., as well as assorted Star Wars warriors and rhinos—and Gordon Ramsey who wimped out earlier.

I meet up with my support team and changed under the Arch then set off for St. Martin's Lane and tapas and plenty of cold beer with Janet, Dick, Ellen, Kyla, Anna (grand-daughter), Phil and Mina (see pic.). Then back to Brum on the 19.17—first class of course! What a day!

Finally, a great day all round with appropriate cool weather for half the course and loads of fantastic support—I lost count of the bands. The knee held up well; in fact, I jogged a few miles from the nineteenth mile and eventually came in 34,635th with almost 2,000 behind me and 30 minutes faster than last year—without crutches!

Hey! It may not be my last marathon after all—but time will tell.

Unfortunately, one of the Everpresents didn't make it, so we're now down to 20!

Dale's time 6 hours 11 minutes 12 seconds. 34,635th

Official finishers 36,524.

Marathon 85 Charity 'Thanks for Life' End Polio Now campaign. Amount raised £808.20

Thanks to all my Rotarian friends, Midlands Fretted Orchestra, Fircones French group, friends, neighbours and family.

April 2010. Dale (Galloping Gourmet) Lyons

London Marathon Report—
Dateline Blackheath Common 17 April 2011

Not So Much A Gallop—More A Stagger!

Why do I put myself through this 26.2 miles torture every year? I can't really think of a good reason other than wanting to be the last Everpresent standing, which is highly unlikely especially as the youngest (and fastest) is nearly 20 years younger. Oh yes! Sponsoring charities is I suppose a very good reason—about £50k raised so far, but it's a pain chasing sponsors after the event!

Mind you, each year we lose 1.5 EPs every year, and this year we lost two, so if I keep marathoning another twelve years, that is, until I'm eighty-six, I could just possibly be the last man standing. We're now down to eighteen! This year I injudiciously decided to toss (a pancake) the 26.2. Having speed-walked the Ashby 20 in a very respectable 3.47 a similar pace plus a bit for the London would give me a finish of 5.15 and almost an hour better than last year.

In the event, I staggered in, in 5.52.29 having run out of steam as early as the fifteen mile mark. So why was I so far out from the plan? Compared to last year, my training plan had been spot on with my Rotary mate Colin Goupillot chivvying me through the races and sub zero training runs around Birminghams canals and Edgbaston Reservoir—thanks Colin. So where did I go wrong?

Was it the heat on the day? It wasn't that fearsome. Did I over-train? The forty mile weeks allowed plenty of pre-marathon recovery time. Did I allow enough rest time? I did chill out two week before in Lanzarote with swimming and a little road work. Was it the effort of tossing? The pancake weighed about 12 ozs, but it didn't feature in my training. Who knows? All I know is from the six mile at Greenwich I knew my target time wasn't on. Anyway enough of my problems, what about the event?

I arrived at the Green start early, at 8 am for the 9.45 kick-off with Dick my mentor. My partner, Janet, was sick and couldn't make her annual pilgrimage in support. Maybe that's another reason? My daughter, Iona, came down from Leeds to cheer on Dad, and so we had a number of group photos.

Me and Dick; Me, Dick, and Iona; Me, Dick, and Dwight Yorke. Yes, really the ex-Villa, Man. Utd stalwart was also running and did a very respectable 3.35—a really nice guy. We almost nabbed Will Young for a photo, but he was too far away. All around the Heath hot air balloons were being fired up, some with observers in the baskets. And a truly enormous balloon of a motorcycle and rider totally dominated the scene—how do they do it? On the ground a brass band played favourites, and we chatted to a female runner in dressed as a carrot, who was going for a Guinness record as the fastest female vegetable—apparently she achieved her target of 4.15 for the record!

Then another group photo with the Everpresents—about eight of the nineteen running. Another Guinness hopeful being interviewed by the BBC was a young man keepy-uppying all the way. This involves, for the uninitiated, keeping a football off the ground all the time whilst 'running' the 26.2. He was being followed by a brass band, who were *playing* whilst walking the 26.2. Obviously they are *not* all locked up yet! No one wanted to interview something as boring as a pancake tosser evidently.

Bang! And it takes me two minutes to get to the start line. This year, the fine weather has brought out masses more than last year. I'm a constant source of amusement with my Galloping Gourmet Chefs hat, and I flip away with reckless abandon in the early stages. Mike Peel, the EP's webmaster catches up at the mile mark, and we chat and run together until the six mile mark at Greenwich when he 'peels' off to see friends. This year, the Cutty Sark is under fire damage repair so we shortcut onto Creek Road through Deptford where a steel band gets in their stride. Assorted debris litter the road, a dead mobile phone, caps, gloves T-shirts, unused power gels, and even pound coins. We turn into Surrey Docks at about nine miles with the first en-route shower to be avoided—can't have the pancake waterlogged! It must be well into the eighties now and no shade. I'm beginning to realise that it's not my day. My pace has slowed to 12.41 at ten miles, and I'm taking on loadsa water with my Hi5 carbo gel. Just beyond the closed Blackwall Tunnel, a big band is playing Glen Miller's 'In The Mood' which I'm definitely *not* in. Every year more and more bands and music line the route which creates a real carnival atmosphere. Rest homes and Care homes along the route bring out their patients for a rare treat and sunbathe for a ring-side seat. They must wonder at the suffering huffers and puffers who still manage to give them a wave. Other viewers offer orange segments and jelly babies along the route.

The pubs spill their drinkers onto the pavement who call out 'toss that flippin pancake Dale'.

The EPs have '31st London and ran every one!' on their vests and T-shirts, so we get lots of 'well done's' and 'amazing' and 'fantastic' and 'unbelievable' and 'incredible'. Some runners slow for a brief chat and some a give a pat on the back, pleased they've actually seen an EP to tell their friends.

Crowds across Tower Bridge hardly leave room for the runners then it's onto the City's Commercial Road. Fast guys are passing us at twenty-one while I'm labouring at the thirteen mile mark with 2.36.51 on the Timex, but still they won't break three hours! In 1986, I was faster at 3.06 for a pancake tossing world record. Ah, happy memories! I try to raise runners' spirits at fifteen miles at the Isle of Dogs underpass with a piercing *ogi, ogi, ogi*—nul response as the 'runners' are hanging on for dear life with still eleven to go! My mile splits have eased up to 13.29 minutes, so I try to raise the pace with a mantra 'only ten to go', 'only nine to go' but despite regular doses of carbo gels my pace slows to 14.09 at the seventeen mile mark. Fortunately, we're into the Canary Wharf complex with a cooling breeze and mega spectator support. The pancake looks pretty good as I do a double flip into the wind.

'Hey remember me, Graham Swann (not the cricketer)?' calls out a runner in clowns gear 'you know, New York 81?' This is a regular marathon meet over the years, and yet I know as little about him now as I did when we met in the '84 London. 'Only six miles to go' I repeat watching the backmarkers struggling through the thirteen mile mark. Another clown collecting in a bucket pushes a supermarket trolley laden with assorted packages and dolls. Behind him the two men London Bus lookalike struggles. Behind them the clearup brigade is champing at the bit, but they'll be out there for another six hours at least! I'm now over four hours into the run and slowing to 15.21 miling retracing the Commercial Road and unlike the early miles a noticeably thin line of runners. Most are walking, few are jogging slowly. Then, through the 35k mark my EP pal Dave Fereday calls 'you're jogging' as he strides past at a metronome twelve minutes milling to finish twenty minutes ahead. I've never in all my marathons been able to do even pace running. At last, downing my last carbo gel and walking at a steady fifteen minutes mile (4 mph) I get a hearty response to another *ogi, ogi, ogi* through the Blackfriars underpass with 2.5 miles to go. It's now over five hours since the start at 9.45, and still the embankment is awash with cheering spectators. They obviously want their money's worth. I can just about manage a few tosses to keep ME going never mind the crowds. So it's under Waterloo Bridge, past Cleo's Needle, under Hungerford Bridge, past the twenty-five mile balloons, right at Westminster Bridge, Big Ben, and Parliament Square (no protestors). Birdcage Walk seems endless abutting

St. James Park, and there's no hiding from the cheering crowds with half a mile to go. So I stop briefly passing Buckingham Palace, no Queen again, and raise a prolong cheer with a triple flip then it's down the Mall for the last 200 and the glorious finish at 5.52.29. I even get a cheery mention from the loudspeaker as I cross the computer mat. The volunteers chorus a 'well done'; on goes the 31st medal and off comes the timing chip—no chip no time. I grab a goody bag and look for my baggage bus—luckily the first one. There's precious few bags left as I totter to a seat outside the St. John's first aid centre. 'My wife's in there' a seated runner points inside the marquee, 'but she's all right,' he laments.

After two bottles of water, I manage to remove a sock and discover an enormous blood blister on my toe. 'Would you like that seen too?' asks a St. John's volunteer. 'No thanks,' I reply, 'it's too far to walk in my delicate state'. Slowly I change, beset with leg, foot, and thigh cramps and set off gingerly for our meeting place at the Cancer Research reception. Well, at least I was twenty minutes faster than last year, and I wasn't tossing which is some consolation. And, more importantly and thanks to my Rotarians, friends, neighbours, and family, around £1,400 has been sponsored for Alzheimers Trust and Cancer Research UK.

CODA The Cancer reception team are entirely gobsmacked with my 'achievement' and offer food, a massage and tea—I thank them and take the tea and an official photo. Dick, Ellen, and shortly after Iona, my daughter, arrive, and after a brief sunning on the terrace, we meander to Rossi's restaurant in the Haymarket for a well-earned ice-cold beer and meal. I feel I've earned it! After 86, is it the last marathon? No. Next up the Keilder Water marathon and the 32nd London in Olympic year—roll on!

Finish time 5.52.19. Position 31,101 with 3,609 behind me! Male winner 2.04.19.

Keilder Marathon Northumbria, 9 October 2011
'Water, Water Everywhere'

If you like rain, high winds, unremitting inclines, and declines and spectacular views (but only when the mist lifts), this is the marathon for you. Just over 1,000 hardy souls participated—they hoped for 3,000—many of them first timers (I'll bet they'll be regretting it today). This 26.2 mile circular hilly course around the man-made reservoir was the brain child of Steve Cram, a bronze medal Olympian and 1,500 metre World Record Holder, now in its second year. Keilder is a national park area about thirty miles north west of Newcastle and boasts loadsa red squirrels and sea eagles in a tourist area bursting with biking, sailing, walking, bird watching, fishing, and, of course, running opportunities. There's even a regular ferry service around the seven mile long stretch—cancelled on marathon day due to high winds and white caps. We stayed at the tiny village of Otterburn fifteen miles away at the Percy Arms a cosy ancient Inn, very friendly but badly in need of TLC & serious renovation. The race organisation could not be faulted with buses shuttling the runners and groupies from the car parks to the Leaplish Waterside Park start where huge marquees dispensed snacks, drinks, a baggage park, loos, a running gear shop, and even free massages. 'Have you done this before?' I asked another runner, 'Yes,' he said, 'and last week I did a forty-four miles cross country race'. '*Last week?*' I repeated, thinking, what better pre-marathon preparation that was. Obviously, they're not all locked up yet! The transfer shuttle hold-ups delayed the start but off went the gun at 10.30 a.m. to start us on a warm up lap around the centre and give the groupies a close view of hardened athletes—and a last chance for up to seven hours (the cut off time). The route was a continuous series of steep inclines and declines either through woods and forests or with occasional glimpses of the choppy water. Even when the rain stopped, albeit briefly, the strong winds shook down heavy showers from the laden branches. Ill advisedly I'd removed my black bin bag cover after six miles just as the wind picked up. Fortunately, the air temperature was a mild 18 °C. My speedwalking style allowed for overtaking on the inclines only to be passed by the same 'runners' on the declines—the tortoise and the hare stories came to mind. Then at nine miles, agony, I felt a blister emerging on my left foot and cursed the new and unwashed sox I'd worn. After a couple of miles, the pain wears off but by eighteen miles I had three more—now three on left and one on the right—I really should know better after eighty-eight marathons! At about seventeen miles, a warming sight. Iona, my youngest daughter, had cycled about ten miles to meet me and do a photoshoot, what a boost. They say marathons start at the twenty-mile mark, and this one had a real sting in the tail. I'd been warned by a runner from last year's race so was prepared. From twenty to the finish, I'd kept up a reasonable pace (for me) around 5 mph, and passed over eighty runners some in dire straits who were barely walking, even on the declines! For the last two miles in the open and a site of the finish heavier rains added to the blister misery, but by then, I was into survival mode, that is, counting each step. Finally looking back, I made a burst for the finish with my team taking photos. Then a lovely young thing hung a beautiful medal and another, two bananas and another, a designer T-shirt and another, a *towel?* And another, a goody bag—my cup runneth over! Janet, my partner said I looked really ill with blue lips—actually, I felt OK until I attempted to change and then just about everything cramped up! I must have put lots more into this one as my finish time of 5.11. 41 was 45 minutes faster than I expected and 40 minutes faster than the London in April! Will I do it again? Well I'll know what to expect but with a 555 miles round trip to Keilder, it's long odds on a rematch! Interesting stats. Finishers 1,109. Last finisher's time 6.41.04. female and 6.37.53 male. Dale's position 928th Time 5 hours 11 minutes 41 seconds. 181 runners *behind me*! My 88th marathon!

Lightning Source UK Ltd.
Milton Keynes UK
UKOW040837250912

199573UK00001B/98/P